Pioneer
Free Will Baptists
Ministers
Burial Locations
In
Michigan

PIONEER FREE WILL BAPTIST MINISTERS BURIAL LOCATIONS IN MICHIGAN

This book was printed in the United States of America.

To order additional copies of this book, contact:
FWB Publications
Enchanting Acres
1006 Rayme Drive
Columbus, Ohio 43207
Alton.loveless@prodigy.net
Or
www.amazon.com

FWB
FWB Publications

Introduction

Michigan

This book represents all that were part of the Free Will Baptist movement, consisting of the Palmer (south), Randall (north) and others such as the Stone, John-Thomas, John Wheeler Assns., NC OFWB and more.

Many of the photos are poor quality, but it was all I could find. Likewise, I do not have photos or tombstones for many of them. The information about these ministers were all that was available to me or found in archives. I made every effort to include those for which they would be remembered. Some I had no information, but research had shown they were of our denomination.

This Section is taken for a two Volume set done by this author.

PIONEER FREE WILL BAPTIST MINISTERS
BURIAL LOCATIONS IN MICHIGAN

Michigan

Benjamin Thomas Abbe
BIRTH
6 Apr 1828
DEATH
27 May 1908 (aged 80)
BURIAL
Oliver Township Cemetery
Elkton, Huron County, Michigan

A Freewill Baptist from Canada served in Michigan.

Rev Able Aldrich
BIRTH   1799
Rhode Island, USA
DEATH   24 Nov 1865 (aged 65–66)
Hadley, Lapeer County, Michigan, USA
BURIAL
Hadley Community Church Cemetery
Hadley, Lapeer County, Michigan, USA
PLOT   90

"Aldrich, Rev. Abel, was converted in Rhode Island, his native state, under the labors of Elder [John] Colby, and later was connected with the Spafford Q.M. (N.Y.), where he was ordained. He soon moved to the West, and united with the Methodist, reuniting with the Free Baptists about 1856. He was a good man, emotional in his preaching. He died in Hadley, Mich., Nov. 24, 1865, aged 67 years."---from "Cyclopedia of Free Baptists," (p.12) pub. 1889, by Burgess and Ward.

Rev Ira Allen
BIRTH   23 Aug 1822
Ohio, USA
DEATH   12 Jun 1895 (aged 72)
Elsie, Clinton County, Michigan, USA
BURIAL
Duplain Township Elsie Village Cemetery
Elsie, Clinton County, Michigan,
Supposedly died while preaching in the pulpit; 1880 census

indicates birth in Ohio, Ira's son William's 1930 census data indicates father's birth in VT; Ira's son William's death certificate indicates Ira's b. in NY.

Rev Lanson Lindley Andrus
BIRTH
22 Oct 1822
Vermont
DEATH   30 Aug 1908 (aged 85)
Saginaw, Saginaw County,
Michigan
BURIAL
Denmark Township Cemetery
Reese, Tuscola County, Michigan
PLOT   4.18

Lanson was a son of Ruel Andrus and his first wife Betsy Lucilda Brown, both of whom were born in Vermont. Ordained to gospel ministry June, 1858.

James Ashley
Birth:
Nov. 18, 1850
Toronto, Ontario, Canada
Death:
Mar. 23, 1882
Cass County, Michigan
Burial:
Adamsville Cemetery,
Adamsville,
Cass County, Michigan,
Plot: Row 7

In 1826 the family removed to Huron County. Ohio, where his father followed farming. In 1841 he was ordained and commenced preaching as a Free Will Baptist minister in the Huron Quarterly Meeting; but most of his pastoral and evangelist work for fourteen years was in new fields where churches were gathered and the Seneca Q.M. was organized. In 1855, he removed to Mason township, Cass county, MI, where he preached at Summerville for twelve years and organized the church at Berrien Center, and preached there nine years. He also did much missionary work and was never idle, working as a carpenter to supply his needs. Through his instrumentality the churches at Adamsville and Mason were built. He labored mostly in the St. Joseph Valley Yearly Meeting where he spent the remainder of his useful life. He was a Representative in the legislature of 1869-70 as a Republican.

REV Franklin Page Augir

Birth:
Oct. 14, 1818
Schuyler
Herkimer County, New York
Death:
Jul. 3, 1893
Springfield
Greene County, Missouri
Burial:
Oak Grove Cemetery,Hillsdale
Hillsdale County, Michigan
Plot: SECTION 14 ROW 3

Franklin, at the age of seventeen, took charge of the transportation of his father's household goods from Sandusky, Ohio, to Racine, Wisconsin, via the lakes, the rest of the family going overland by team. That was before the days of steam navigation, and the boat being unable to make harbor at Racine on the down trip, kept on to Chicago. There Franklin made inquiry at the ferry, the only means of crossing the Chicago river at that time, and found that his father's party had crossed only a few hours before. Hurrying on he overtook them and spent the night with the family. .

He frequently remarked that Chicago at that time was mostly a marsh, and that government land in that locality would hardly be taken as a gift. His father's family made their home in Racine County, Wisconsin, near Honey Creek. .

Franklin was educated at Western Reserve Seminary, Ohio; Whitestown Seminary, NY; and Hillsdale College, Michigan. He was ordained by a Council of the Honey Creek Quarterly Meeting in April 1847. His forty years of active ministry were spent in Rhode Island, Wisconsin, Illinois, Michigan, Iowa, Minnesota, and Kansas. .

For several terms he was on the Board of Trustees of Hillsdale College. .

The leading characteristic of "Elder Augir" as he was familiarly called, was his logical turn of mind. He was absolutely fearless in his search for truth. He was years in advance of his time on many questions, having no fear for religion in the acceptance of newly discovered facts. He strongly combatted the doctrine of the literal resurrection of the body, and believed the second coming of Christ was a spiritual and not an earthly kingdom. He taught the spiritual and not the literal Inspiration of the Scriptures. .

In political opinions he was also a leader and not a follower and was prominent Abolitionist in every community he served during the years of the agitation of that issue. He was a supporter of the Republican Party for thirty years. For the last few years of his life, however, his conviction of the growing domination of the "money power" in the councils of that party and its failure to thoroughly enforce temperance legislation, even when enacted, led him into the Prohibition Party.

He believed and asserted that when men were elected on the issues thus presented they would know that a majority were supporting them and could be relied upon to enforce the laws. History and political economy were his favorite subjects of thought and study. He clearly foresaw many issues that have come up for settlement long in advance of their becoming popular and advocated the right public policy in regard to them.

Haven, Connecticut,

He married Lavina Lillie Bixby Augir (1821 - 1909) and they had the following children: Arvilla Leila Augir (1848 - 1871), Newell Galusha Augir (1849 - 1918), Emmer Estella Augir (1851 - 1871), Wayland Bixby Augir (1853 - 1926), Viola Juliett Augir (1855 - 1954), Addie B Augir (1861 - 1861).

Rev Jeremiah Baldwin
Birth:
1798
Vermont
Death
March 8, 1878
Oakland Co. Michigan
Burial:
Oak Grove Cemetery
Hillsdale
Hillsdale County, Michigan
Plot: SECTION 5 ROW 6

Rev. Jeremiah Baldwin was born in Strafford, VT, in 1798. At the age of nine years he went with his grandfather, Rev. N. Brown, to Bethany, NY. At Ellington, NY, in 1832, he turned out his liquors from his hotel, and soon began to preach. He was licensed the next year, and ordained in 1840. At Ellington he was interested in every good work, especially education, temperance, and the anti-slavery cause. He was a half-brother of Rev. Wm. Johnson, and the father-in-law of Pres.

Fairfield, of Hillsdale College, Michigan, to which place he moved about 1861. A man of great energy and force of character, he was always in earnest, and his convictions were strong and positive.

Rev George E. Barnard
Birth: 1860
Death: 1949
Burial:
Oak Grove Cemetery
Coldwater
Branch County
Michigan, USA

Pastored in Ohio and reported of the Bible Institute in the Central Ohio Yearly Meeting in 1907.

George T. Baxter
Birth:
Jul. 11, 1837
Long Island City
Queens County, New York
Death:
Jul. 16, 1912
Oceana County, Michigan
Burial:
Otto Township Cemetery
Rothbury
Oceana County, Michigan

He was converted in 1878 and labored with success as a licensed preacher among the United Brethren in the White River mission. Afterwards he united with the Free Baptists being connected with the East Otto church of the Holton and White River Quarterly Meeting in the state of Michigan.

His first wife was Mary Mason whom he married in 1859/60?. On May 13, 1866 in Defiance County, Ohio he married Mary Jane Morgan (1847-May 20, 1891 Otto, Oceana Co., Michigan). Mary Jane was born November 22, 1847 Ohio and died May 22, 1891 in Otto, Oceana County, Michigan. Mary's parents were Richard S. Morgan & Margarette A. Then George T. Baxter married Margaret (Harjes) Schmiedeknecht, widow of Phillip.

Archibald Bennet
Birth:
Jan. 22, 1807
Otsego, N.Y.
Death:
Oct. 22, 1889
Waverly, Michigan
Burial:
Covey Hill Cemetery
Van Buren County, Michigan

Archibald Bennet married Harriet C. (Whitcher) Bennet when 25 years of age and began to preach at age 29 receiving his ordination two years later. He labored as a revivalist for seven years in Columbus and vicinity and for four years in North

Clarkson. In about 1849 he moved to Michigan where he ministered and organized Free Will Baptist churches. He was engaged in about 20 revivals and saw over 1000 conversions and baptized several hundred.At his death he was 61 yrs, 9 mos.

Rev James Bignall
Birth:
1799
Pittstown
Rensselaer County, New York
Death:
Aug. 3, 1869
Lyons
Ionia County, Michigan
Burial:
Lapham Cemetery
Salem
Washtenaw County, Michigan

Rev. James Bignal was baptized by Eld. Wire [Samuel] in 1820, and in 1828, he was ordained by the Holland Purchase Y.M. of Freewill Baptists, at Potter, NY.

His early labors were in western New York and northern Pennsylvania. The esteem in which he was held is evinced by his serving as a delegate from Holland Purchase Yearly Meeting to the General Conference of 1831 and 1835 from NY and PA, Yearly Meetings in that of 1844. One of the two last named he was made ass't moderator. The Conference Hymn Book was published by him in the early years and ran through several additions. In 1844, he moved to Ingraham Co. MI where he labored ten years. After this he continued the work until his death. Bro. Bignal associated with Revs David Marks, Samuel Wire, and others, enduring the hardships of the itinerant period joyfully that he might win souls. He was a safe counselor, a good disciplinarian, sometimes pronounced "ahead of the times" and never a laggard in any good work. His children are useful members of the church."

He was married to Sarah KNAPP. She was in the Free Will Baptist Church in Barrington, NY, which her father, Matthew KNAPP, was instrumental in organizing. He served as a deacon and then later, was voted by Y.M.(Yearly Meeting) to license him to preach.

Rev George P. Blanchard
Birth:
Dec. 28, 1835
Vermont
Death:
Jun. 10, 1907
Alma
Gratiot County
Michigan
Burial:
Riverside Cemetery
Alma
Gratiot County, Michigan
Plot: P

Rev. G.P. Blanchard was born in Vermont, Dec. 28, 1833. He married Mary A. Beers, Sept. 27, 1860, and has two children.

He studied at Whitestown Seminary 1856-57, also later at Hillsdale College, in the College and Theological departments. He received license to preach in 1853 and was ordained in 1860. His pastorates were at Rome and Cambridge, Mich.; Chicago, Ill; Paw Paw, Mich; Providence (Roger Williams church), R.I., and Harrisburg, PA. He also held revival meetings in Pittsford, Mich, and Hamlin, N.Y., and baptized 238 converts." Civil War Veteran. (GAR)
53rd Massachusetts infantry, Co. Sergeant) Enlisted 15 Sept 1862. is charged 17 July 1863.
Son of Abijah Blanchard and Eda Nurse. m 27 Sep 1860 Lenawee Co., MI. Mary Ann Beers (15 Feb 1839 MI - 10 Dec 1920 Alma, MI)dau of Jabez Beers and Sarah Langden

Rev Lucius Darwin Boynton
Birth:
Oct. 20, 1846
New York
Death:
Apr. 7, 1917
Pontiac
Oakland County
Michigan
Burial:
Oak Hill Cemetery
Pontiac
Oakland County
Michigan
Plot: Section 9

Married twice, first to Marnlla Marks Reyolds, second to Armintha Pugsley.

Lucius was a Baptist Minister and migrated from New York, living at times in Ohio, Illinois, and mostly in Michigan.

Boynton, Rev. Lucius D., was born Oct. 20, 1846, at Bethany, N. Y. where his parents, Ezra and Mary (Darwin) Boynton, resided. He consecrated his life to God in May, 1863; was educated at Hillsdale College; received license in 1872, and was ordained Sept. 17, 1876. His pastorates have been at Blackberry, (Elburn) Ill., Auburn, O., Wellsburg, Pa., Colebrook, O., and Paw Paw, Mich. He is now ministering to the Gliddensburg, Arlington, and Oshtemo churches, of the Van Buren Q. M., Mich. He has baptized forty-nine converts. Dec. 31, 1874, he was married to Marilla M. Reynolds; they now have three children to brighten their home.

George Bradley
Birth:
May 28, 1830
Death:
Aug. 8, 1900
Hillsdale,
Michigan
Burial:
Oak Grove Cemetery
Hillsdale
Hillsdale County,
Michigan

Attended Michigan Central College, and was a professor at Oberlin College and Hillsdale College. Ordained at North Parsonsfield , Me., July 5, 1860. He pastored in Maine, Wisconsin, Iowa, Indiana and Kansas. He was a trustee of Hillsdale College and western editor of *The Morning Star*. Spouse: Sally Ann Weaver Bradley (1834 - 1913).

David Daniel Brown
Birth:
1822
Ontario, Canada
Death:
Aug. 3, 1869
Macomb County, Michigan
Burial:

Centennial Cemetery
New Haven, Macomb County,
Michigan

Rev. Brown was an ordained Freewill Baptist minister, baptized by Rev. S. Griffith, and ordained in 1845, after which he moved to Lexington, MI and preached in the Oxford Quarterly Meeting, with considerable success, and in June, 1867, settled as pastor of the Bruce Church, where he remained until his death in Bruce Twp of Macomb County, Michigan, when forty-seven years of age. He is recorded as having served in Michigan's 22nd Reg. Inf., Co. K, from 1864-1865, mustering out at Murfreesboro, TN, from the 29th Inf. Reg. having previously transferred from 22nd to 29th. It's possible he contracted his "consumption", i.e. TB, while exposed in the War.

Inscription:
Died Aug 3, 1869
Aged 47 yrs. 4 mos. 29 days

Here he will sleep till that great day when Heaven and earth shall pass away when saints with joy their graves forsake.

William C. Burns
Birth:
1854
Death:
1955
Burial:
Macon Cemetery
Macon
Lenawee County, Michigan

He was converted in 1868 and was ordained to the ministry in 1880 and was a minister to the churches at Paw Paw, Michigan and Fairport, New York. He baptized 35 converts during his ministry and has been active in the Young Peoples Society Of

Christian Endeavor and served as an instructor in history at Oak Park Seminary in Paw Paw, Michigan. On September 9, 1885 he married Alice Collins. His education was received at Hillsdale College and the Theological School. He also did postgraduate work at Auburn Theological Seminary in New York.

Because He Rose, We Too Shall Rise.

John Jay Butler
Birth:
Apr. 9, 1814
Berwick,
York County, Maine
Death:
Jun. 16, 1891

Hillsdale,
Hillsdale County,
Michigan
Burial:
Oak Grove Cemetery,
Hillsdale,
Hillsdale County,
Michigan,
Plot: Sect. 15 - Row 5

Prof. John J. Butler, when quite young became interested in politics and religion. He united with the Free Will Baptist church of Great Falls, NH. When the Free Will Baptists established a Seminary at Parsonsfield, ME, he became a student and prepared for college. While there he lived with the family of Rev. George Lamb, an eminent minister of the village, for whom he formed a deep attachment and under whose direction he began holding meetings and delivering addresses. John was ordained a minister in 1846. He was Professor Emeritus of Systematic Theology in the early Free Will Baptist movement in New England. He graduated at Bowdoin College in 1837. Following his graduation, he began teaching as an assistant teacher in the Seminary in Parsonsfield. In Dec. 1839, he entered Andover Theological Sem. Mass. The highlights of his teaching career included holding the professorship of systematic theology in the Whitestown Seminary at Whitestown, New York for 10 years, as well as holding the professorship of systematic theology in the

Seminary at New Hampton, New Hampshire for 16 years, and in Bates College at Lewiston, Maine for 3 years. In 1860, Bowdoin College gave him the degree of Doctor of Divinity. In 1873, Butler took the chair of Hebrew Language and Literature at Hillsdale College, in Michigan. A large number of his pupils became worthy ministers and missionaries abroad. No less than fifteen hundred pupils were under his instruction, and a third prepared for the Gospel ministry. He retired from teaching in Hillsdale in 1883.He was the author of: Natural and Revealed Theology (Dover, New Hampshire, 1861) Commentary on the Gospels (1870) Commentary on the Acts, Romans, and First and Second Corinthians. (1871) Lectures on systematic theology: embracing the existence and attributes of God, the authority and doctrine of the scriptures, the institutions and ordinances of the gospel (with Ransom Dunn, 1892) In 1834, Dr. Butler became the assistant editor of The *Morning Star*, a Free Will Baptist publication.

Missionary Julia Emma *Phillips* Burkholder
Birth:
Jun. 5, 1845,
India
Death:
1931
Dickinson County, Michigan
Burial:
Oak Grove Cemetery,
Hillsdale,
Hillsdale County, Michigan

Julia Emma was the daughter of Jeremiah Phillips, D.D., and Hannah (Cummings) Phillips, missionaries for the Free Will Baptist church. She was one of six of their children to serve in

India. She was born in Jelasore, India, Orissa Province. She was married to Thomas Wesley Burkholder, M.D., Nov. 8, 1879, by her brother, James Liddell Phillips, M.D., in India. She and her husband as a physician served many years in India, where he died and is buried, as well as her brother, Dr. James L. Phillips, and her mother, Hannah Cummings Phillips. Julia E. studied at Hillsdale College, Michigan, and served as missionary in India from 1865-1917. Her father, Jeremiah, is bur. in Oak Grove, as well as sisters, Ida Orissa, Mary Anne Platt(s) and bro.-in-law, Dr. Richard Gilbert Platt(s), M.D., and other kindred.

Inscription:
Missionary to India
1865-1917

Rev. Ruth Hunt Cilley
Birth:
Nov. 18, 1819
Vermont

Death:
Aug. 7, 1878
Burial:
Idlewild Cemetery
Kent City
Kent County, Michigan,

Wife of Rev. Elbridge G Cilley b. NH 1818. It was written of her that "she was a helpmeet indeed, sharing the joys, sorrows and burdens of a pioneer minister's life, being especially active in Sabbath-school work." She was mother of five children, four living to adult-hood, one, "Mrs. Z.F. Griffin of India."
Children:
Calvin B b. VT 1846 (This might also be D. Dexter from the 1860 census)-Elizabeth (Libbie) b. MI 1851-Naomi S b. MI 1855 Simeon H b. MI 1861

Dudley E Clark
Birth:
Jul. 18, 1855
Ashtabula County, Ohio
Death:
Nov. 24, 1884 Arlington,
Rhode Island
Burial:
Northlawn Cemetery,
North Adams,
Hillsdale County, Michigan

He was graduated at Hillsdale College, Mich., in 1879, and from the Theological Department of this college in 1881. He was ordained in 1880, and preached while in school, at Woodstock, Mich., where he witnessed a revival and a score of conversions. After his graduation he preached and taught school at Davison Station, Mich., where his labors were highly esteemed. In 1883, he was called to Arlington, R.I., where he endeared himself to many in the short time before his early death.

Elijah Cook
Birth:
Jul. 17, 1793
Rensselaer County,
New York
Death:
Jan. 31, 1872
Eckfor, Calhoun County,
Michigan
Burial:
Cook's Prairie Cemetery
Clarendon,
Calhoun County,
Michigan

Cook, Rev. Elijah, of Cook's Prairie, Mich., died aged 78 years. He was converted when fourteen, and soon moved from Oneida County; N. Y., to Clarkson, where his home welcomed the fathers of those times.

In 1835 he moved to Michigan, locating at Cook's Prairie, where he saw the need of ministerial labor and took up the work. He was ordained in 1845, and his zealous labors were crowned with success. About 1858 he united with the Girard church. He and his companion of fifty-seven years were highly esteemed.

Ellen A Cross Copp
Birth:
1849
Death:
December 23, 1924
Waterloo, N. Y.
Burial:
Oak Grove Cemetery
Hillsdale
Hillsdale County, Michigan
Plot: SECTION 16 ROW 1

Rev. Ellen A. Copp died at the home of her daughter, Mr. A. C. Price, at seventy-five years and 9 months of age. She was buried in Hillsdale, Michigan beside her. She was a pastor of the Free Baptist Church in this city for a time and has many friends in Evansville.

January 8, 1925, *Evansville Review*, p. 3, col. 5, Evansville, Wisconsin.

Her spouse was Rev. John Scott Copp (1843 - 1896).

Mrs. Copp was a teacher and religious leader, well respected. Taught for a time in the Freewill Baptist College in Tecumseh, OK, in 1920's. Randall University has a Latin New Testament, with her name on inside cover showing it was from her "Home Library."

Rev John Scott Copp
Birth:
Jan. 17, 1843
Saint Albans
Somerset County, Maine
Death:
Jun. 19, 1896
Hillsdale
Hillsdale County, Michigan
Burial:
Oak Grove Cemetery
Hillsdale
Hillsdale County, Michigan
Plot: SECTION 16 ROW 1

Prof. John Scott Copp, A.M., was the 2nd of four children of John B. and Cyrena Mills COPP, both of Maine. His mother, Cyrena, was sister of Judge C.B. Mills, of Tuscola Co. MI. Rev. Copp's parents resided in ME until 1847, when they moved to Ohio, Ashtabula Co. His father and grandfather [Roger Copp] were both faithful ministers in the Freewill Baptist denomination.

John B. Copp, father, died in Genesee Co. MI in 1855 and his mother had died after a short illness, in Ohio in 1852.

Rev. J. S. Copp had labored with others in the abolition of slavery. He joined the 16th Mich Inf., Co. C, in the Civil War, and served until he suffered severe wounds at Battle of Bull Run, which soon after he was discharged. His superiors cited him for bravery and good conduct.

After his discharge he returned to Mich., and was ordained in 1868. He and entered Hillsdale College taking classical courses and graduated in 1869. He then entered Andover Theological Seminary near Boston, MA, and graduated in 1872.

He then accepted a professorship at Hillsdale College, MI, taking charge of the Dept. of Hebrew Languages, Literature and Church History, which position he held 3 yrs. During 1882-83, he attended lectures at Universities of Berlin and Heidelberg,

Germany, on Literature, Philosophy and Theology. He also was professor of Systematic Theology of Hillsdale Theology Dept.

He was married in 1874 to Miss Ellen A. CROSS, of Wis. They had three children, 2 sons, 1 daugh.

Prof. Copp was elected in 1886 a member of the Modern Language Ass'n of America.

--from Univ.of Mich County Histl., Portraits & Biography Album...of Prominent and Representative Citizens, Pub. Ann Arbor, Mich, 1888.

The Divine Power Appears Fearful In Its Holiness

Rev Andrew Jackson Davis
BIRTH
30 Oct 1829
Webster, Monroe County, New York
DEATH
24 Sep 1903 (aged 73)
Hillsdale, Hillsdale County, Michigan
BURIAL
Oak Grove Cemetery

Hillsdale, Hillsdale County, Michigan
PLOT   SECTION 13 ROW 16

Ordained 1854 and was a useful minister/pastor and leader.

Rev Jairus Eaton Davis
Birth:
Feb. 13, 1813
Quebec, Canada
Death:
Dec. 2, 1870
Reading
Hillsdale County
Michigan
Burial:
Oak Grove Cemetery
Hillsdale
Hillsdale County
Michigan
Plot: SECTION 2 ROW 5

Ordained 1834 in Ohio Ashtabula Q.M. and was active in western states and engaged for years in the Freewill Baptist work.

Rev James Harvey Darling
Birth:
Dec. 2, 1828
Spafford
Onondaga County
New York
Death:
Jul. 31, 1916
Paw Paw
Van Buren County
Michigan
Burial:
Covey Hill Cemetery
Van Buren County
Michigan

Died at age 87 yrs, 7 months and 29 days. His parents were Rev. Jacob W. Darling (1800-1868) and Mary (Buffington) Darling. He studied at Cortland Academy, Homer, N.Y., and at the Biblical School at Whitestown, a Free Will Baptist institution. His father was also a FWB minister, having died in Eleroy, Ill.

James' life was consecrated to God in 1848, and the same year license to preach was granted. He was ordained a Free Will Baptist minister by Rev. R. Ide and others, Sept. 20, 1853. After ministering to the Spafford and Summerhill churches, N.Y., he moved to Michigan, where the remainder of his ministry, except three years at Prairie Centre and Homer, Ill., has been spent. He has ministered to the Summerville, Paw Paw, Waverly, Oshtemo, Gliddengurg, Arlington, Gobleville, Porter and Ortonville churches, enjoying revivals in them all. He has (by 1889) organized three churches and baptized over one hundred converts. On March 26, 1851, he was married to Mary M. French, and has three children, three having died.

Mary died sometime after 1890, and he married Lavella (or Lovenel) in 1894, and had a son, Jacob W, 2 yrs in the 1900 census.

Rev Egbert Oakley Dickinson

Birth:
Aug. 31, 1844
Ellenville
Ulster County
New York
Death:
Mar. 26, 1928
Hillsdale
Hillsdale County
Michigan
Burial:
Oak Grove Cemetery
Hillsdale
Hillsdale County, Michigan

Son of Phineas/Finis and Julia Ann Melendy/Maloney Dickinson

Civil War Veteran-Pvt,Co C 4th MI CAV

Dickinson, Rev. E. O., son of Finis and Julia An n (Melendy) Dickinson, was born at Ulchester, N. Y., Aug. 31, 1844· He was married to J. Ella Cook June 22, 1875. After a preparatory course of education at Paw Paw, Mich., he entered Hillsdale College and was graduated from the classical and theological departments in I 875· His pastorates have been Bedford, Wixom and Greenville, Mich., and Haw- patch, Wolf Lake and Ridgeville, Ind. The churches were blessed with revivals, and many were baptized during his pastorates. In the war of the Rebellion, he served three years in the Union army. He became president of Ridgeville College, Indiana, in June, 1886.

Edward John Doyle

Birth:
Nov. 11, 1831
Nova Scotia
Canada
Death:
Oct. 27, 1889
Burial:
Capac Cemetery
Capac
St. Clair County
Michigan
Plot: CAPAC-OLD-20-4

His parents were M.S. and Sarah (Tuffs) Doyle. He was given a license to the gospel ministry in August 1861, and in July 1862, he received ordination in the Freewill Baptist church. He labored with the Oxford Quarterly Meeting in Mich., twenty-six years, eight years acting as clerk; he has also been a member of the Mission Board fifteen years. He has conducted a large number of revivals, baptizing about two thousand converts, and has organized nine churches. His eldest son, A.F. Doyle, is principal of a high school.

devoted to her husband's success and to her home. She was a quiet and gracious lady in her church and in the Hillsdale College circle.

(She shares a double stone with her husband, and a footstone with "Mother" inscribed on it.

Inscription:
"Together They labored Here-
They Rest Together There--
Forever With The Lord."

Cyrena Emery Emery Dunn
Birth:
Feb. 20, 1824
Maine
Death:
May 20, 1896
Hillsdale
Hillsdale County
Michigan
Burial:
Oak Grove Cemetery
Hillsdale
Hillsdale County
Michigan
Plot: SECTION 5 ROW 3

Cyrena Emery mar. Rev. Ransom Dunn, in 1849, in Dover, New Hampshire. They had several children, some died as young children. She was hostess many times at Hillsdale College where her husband was professor and then President. She was eulogized as a woman who was

Dr Ransom Dunn
Birth:
Jul. 7, 1818
Bakersfield,
Franklin County, Vermont
Death:
Nov. 9, 1900
Scranton,
Lackawanna Cty,
Pennsylvania,
Burial:
Oak Grove Cemetery,
Hillsdale, Hillsdale County,
Michigan,
Plot: Sect 5, Lot 150

He grew up in Vermont one of ten children of John and Abigail Dunn. All four of their sons became ministers, including Ransom. His eyesight was poor but he never ceased to study. He became an orator, writer and sought-after pastor in the northeastern Free Will Baptist movement. He came west to preach and teach in the newer states, finally lending his time and influence to the growth of Hillsdale College in its formative years, and forward. He became the "Grand Ole Man" of Hillsdale College, serving the College in various capacities (professor, fund-raiser, and president) from 1852 to 1900. From 1853 to 1855, he obtained over $10,000 of the original college funding by travelling 6,000 miles by carriage through frontier Illinois, Wisconsin, Iowa and Minnesota. Dr. Dunn was a long-time anti-slavery activist. In 1891, a book of lectures by Prof. Dunn, and co-educator Prof. Butler entitled, *"Butler and Dunn's Systematic Theology"*, was published, which instantly became a favorite of scholars interested in biblical doctrines, and is still a sought-after volume. Within the cornerstone of Central Hall is the prayer of Ransom Dunn: "May earth be better and heaven richer because of the life and labor of Hillsdale College." He had extensive work in Ohio at Geauga Seminary and Rio Grande College where he was the first president.

Francis Wayland Dunn
Birth:
Jan. 29, 1843 Ohio
Death:
Dec. 13, 1874
Hillsdale
Hillsdale County
Michigan
Burial:
Oak Grove Cemetery Hillsdale
Hillsdale County
Michigan

The second son of Rev. Dr. Ransom Dunn. He graduated from Hillsdale College in 1862, and went into the 64th Reg. of Illinois Volunteers for the War, along with his brother, Newell Ransom. They served in Mississippi, going thru several battles, and when his brother died of typhoid fever, he was with him and took responsibility to ship the body back to Hillsdale. After the war he became editor of *The Christian Freeman*, a denominational publication. His health continued to decline from the exposures of war. 'He accepted the chair of belles letters at Hillsdale, but it was only a matter of months until his brief professorship would end.' He suffered from tuberculosis and died in 1874, an outstanding young man, loved by his family and college friends.

Wellington DePuy
Birth:
Aug. 20, 1849
Mount Morris
Livingston County, New York
Death:
Mar. 22, 1919
Grand Ledge
Eaton County, Michigan
Burial:
Oakwood Cemetery
Eaton Rapids
Eaton County, Michigan

He graduated from Hillsdale College, Michigan in 1878. He had been converted in 1872 and license by the Hillsdale Quarter Meeting in 1876. In 1880 he graduated from Bates Theological School, Lewiston, Maine and in April 1881 he settled in Ortonville, Michigan. On December 11, 1881 he was ordained to the Free Will Baptists ministry. In 1882 he became the pastor of the Grand Ledge, Michigan church and thereafter became a Congregationalist in 1885.

Gilbert G. Durfee
Birth:
Unknown
New York
Death:
Dec. 23, 1868
Burial:
Forest Home Cemetery
Greenville, Montcalm County,
Michigan, Plot: sec 7

He affiliated with the Free Baptists in Michigan in 1865, but due to failing health, soon had to retire from active ministry. Ordained Freewill Baptist minister, bn NY, abt 1819, moved to Michigan, where he died relatively young.

Rev Abner C Eggleston
Birth:
1808
Ulysses
Tompkins County
New York
Death:
Jun. 16, 1864
Lawrence
Van Buren County
Michigan
Burial:
Wildey Cemetery
Paw Paw

Van Buren County
Michigan
Plot: Section A Row 8 Position 4
Lot A35

Rev. Abner C. Eggleston died aged 56 years. He was licensed while in NY, but in about a year moved to Illinois, and was ordained by the Walnut Creek Quarterly Meeting (QM). He traveled as a pioneer minister in the southwestern part of the state, where he gathered several churches. In 1849 he removed to the Van Buren QM (Michigan), and organized other churches. He was devoted and successful in his work for the Master.

Nathaniel Ewer
Birth:
1800
Death:
Aug. 9, 1836
Burial:
Perry McFarlen Cemetery
Grand Blanc
Genesee County, Michigan

An ordained Freewill Baptist pioneer minister from Vermont. Died young.

Micaiah Fairfield
Birth:
Apr. 3, 1786
Vermont
Death:
Feb. 19, 1858
Burial:
Oak Grove Cemetery
Hillsdale
Hillsdale County Michigan

Micaiah Fairfield graduated Middlebury College, VT, with highest honors, and studied theology at Andover, Mass. His roommates there were Judson, Newell and Rice, and no one of the number was more devoted to missionary work than he. One of their children was Rev. Edmund Burke Fairfield, D.D., LL.D, who became president (1848) of Hillsdale College, Hillsdale, MI. Rev. Micaiah Fairfield, was for fifty years engaged in the work of the ministry, and whether missionary or pastor, his aim was for the promotion of the gospel.

Rev Jessie Calvin Ferris
Birth:
Dec. 31, 1817
Smyrna
Chenango County
New York
Death:
Jul. 17, 1901
Lansing
Ingham County
Michigan
Burial:
Mount Hope Cemetery
Lansing
Ingham County
Michigan

His parents were Robert R. and Abigail (Lindley) Ferris. He experienced religion in December, 1837, was licensed to preach in 1847; studied at the Biblical School at Whitestown, N.Y., and received ordination Feb. 15, 1849. His pastorates have been with the Smyrna and Galen and Savannah churches, in New York, and the Lansing and Orange churches in Michigan.

The DeWitt church was gathered through his instrumentality, and he has assisted in revivals at Bath, Elsie, Delta, and other places with good results. He now [1889] resides at North Lansing, Mich.

William Penson Fifield
Birth:
Jul. 7, 1813
Salisbury,
Merrimack County,
New Hampshire
Death:
Feb. 12, 1880
Jackson County, Michigan
Burial:
Fifield Cemetery,
Blackman Township,
Jackson Cty, Michigan

William P. Fifield came to Michigan with his parents, Enoch and Abigail (Stevens) Fifield, in 1830, locating on a farm near Jackson. He united with the Baptists in 1834, but shortly afterward became connected with the Freewill Baptists. He firmly maintained the principles he so dearly loved to the end. He was deeply interested in all the denominational work.

Ebenezer Fisk
Birth:
Oct. 1, 1802
Death:
Oct. 5, 1890
Jackson, Michigan
Burial:
Oak Grove Cemetery
Hillsdale
Hillsdale County, Michigan

He studied at New Hampton institution and was ordained there in 1836. His ministry was mainly in NH and area before moving to Michigan. He was s revival preacher and good pastor. He was president of the Anti-slavery Society, 1848. Trustee of the Printing Establishment and one of the Corporators. He was a member of the Executive Committee for seven years. He was one of the founders of the New Hampton Literary Institution and first president of its Board of Trustees. He was twice a member of the General Conference. He represented New Hampton in the Legislature.

Henry Mead Ford
Birth:
Apr., 1853
Hillsdale
Hillsdale County,
Michigan
Death:
Jun. 3, 1946
Brooklyn
Jackson County,
Michigan
Burial:
Oak Grove Cemetery
Hillsdale
Hillsdale County,
Michigan
Plot: SECTION 19E
ROW 19EW

Rev Spencer J. Fowler
Birth:
Feb. 1, 1825
Groveland
Livingston County
New York,
Death:
Aug. 28, 1875
Saco, York County, Maine
Burial:
Oak Grove Cemetery
Hillsdale
Hillsdale County, Michigan
Plot: SECTION 2 ROW 4

His spouse was Sarah Beecher Searle Ford (1856 - 1933) and they has son Robert Darwin Ford (1888 - 1931).

Stimulated by the kind words of a lady from Oberlin, OH, assuring him that it was possible, he without aid beyond the gift of a single dollar, fitted for college, and spent two years at Hamilton, one at Yale, where he distinguished himself in mathematics, and one at Union, graduating in 1849. The next year he was married in Geneva, OH, to Miss Elizabeth M. Crawford.

He was connected with Geauga Seminary, OH, for a time, and in 1850 took charge of the academy in Kingsville, OH, continuing there four years. He had consecrated himself to God when eleven years of age and was ordained in 1857.

The chief work of his life was in connection with Hillsdale College. In 1856 he entered upon his duties as professor of mathematics and natural philosophy, a position which he filled with credit until his death. Casting his lot with the college in its infancy at a time when its existence depended upon the sacrifice of its servants, it may be truly said his life was given to the cause of Christian education. He was a man of more than ordinary energy and consecration to his life work. He never shirked any duty, but in the class room, in the faculty meeting, as a trustee and as member of the prudential committee, was always prompt, accurate and efficient, respected by his associates and loved for his kind helpfulness. Added to his manifold duties in the college, the meager salary then paid compelled him to serve also as pastor of neighboring churches, and in this capacity also he was useful. He acted also as solicitor in raising funds for the college and added more than $20,000 to its endowment funds. These incessant labors so affected his health that, in 1875, he requested leave of absence from college duties, and seeking rest near the sea, after a short illness he died at Saco, Maine, Aug. 28, in the fifty-first year of his age. In his early death the students, the college and the denomination sustained a great loss."

Rev Howard M. Freeman
BIRTH
15 Jul 1842
Pittsfield , Maine
DEATH
10 Sep 1929 (aged 87)
Sparta, Kent County, Michigan
BURIAL
Greenwood Cemetery
Sparta, Kent County, Michigan

Freeman, Rev. Howard M., son of Jacob and Mary Hodgekins Freeman. He was married in 1880 to Ella L Meeker. He turned to God in 1863 and was licensed in 1878, and was ordained by the Grand Rapids, (MI) Quarterly Meeting in 1881, he has held two pastorates and is now [1888] connected with the Lisbon church."--from "Free Baptist Cyclopedia," pub. 1889, by Burgess and Ward.

Retire W. Frees, Jr
Birth:
Jan. 2, 1864
Wisconsin
Death:
Feb. 5, 1937
Ypsilanti
Washtenaw County
Michigan
Burial:
Sand Creek Cemetery
Lenawee County
Michigan

Newton Preston Gates
Birth:
Feb. 18, 1894
Clay County, Arkansas
Death:
Nov. 1, 1977
Detroit,
Wayne County, Michigan
Burial:
Roseland Park Cemetery,
Berkley, Oakland County,
Michigan

FREES, Rev. R. W. [Retire W. Jr], 1864-1937, b. Wisconsin, d. Mich. He is bur in Sand Creek Cem. Lenawee Co. MI. He was an ordained minister, and a dth cert.

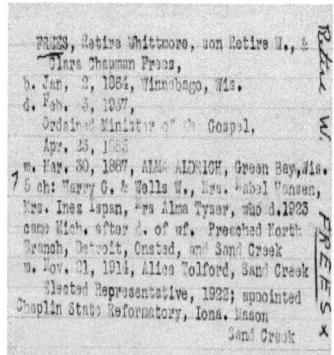

He was the founder of the First Free Will Baptist Church in Hazel Park, which was the very first Free Will Baptist Church in the state of Michigan after the 1935 merger of the present FWB Natl' Association. He was the founder of the Liberty Association of Free Will Baptist churches in the state and was founder of the Free Will Baptist Temple in Detroit. He was widely known as a song writer and singer. He was awarded the Professor of Music degree from the Arkansas State Normal Music College. His daughter, Winona, married Raymond Riggs which continued a large legacy of FWB ministers.

Alba A Glovier

Birth:
Dec. 23, 1856
New Hampshire
Death:
Dec. 7, 1933
Chicago
Cook County
Illinois
Burial:
Mount Evergreen Cemetery
Jackson
Jackson County
Michigan
Plot: Sec C Lot 107

he was married to Mary Elizabeth Glovier (1861 - 1940)* Parents, J H and L S (McCullock) Glovier, b. in East Landaff, NH, Dec. 22, 1856. He mar. Miss Etta P. Farr, who d. two yrs later. "Bro. Glovier is now pursuing a course of theological study at Hillsdale College with the ministry in view."

Alpheus P "Cephas" Goodrich

BIRTH
1810
New York,
DEATH 20 Jun 1893 (aged 82–83)

Metamora, Lapeer County, Michigan
BURIAL Unknown
Ordained a Freewill Baptist minister in Aug. 1834. He exerted a wide influence for good in eastern Michigan where he was honored as one of the "Fathers."

Thomas Grinnell

Birth:
1794
Exeter
Washington County, Rhode Island
Death:
Feb. 4, 1882
Bethel
Branch County, Michigan
Burial:
Snow Prairie Cemetery
Bethel
Branch County, Michigan

A native of Exeter, R. I., died at age 89 years. Shortly after his marriage he made his home in Genesee County, N.Y., where he was ordained in 1826. Two years later he moved to Chautauqua County, where his ministry was marked by persevering efforts for the cause he loved. Later he labored in Wisconsin and Illinois, making his home in Michigan.
Note: *Chautauqua Co. NY history:* The Free-Will Baptist Church, in the town of Cherry Creek, was formed about the year 1826, by Rev Thomas Grinnell; and is said to have been the earliest religious organization in the town.

Ordained in June 1872, by the Michigan Yearly Meeting, after his return from the army.

John Hallack served in Co.L, 8th Michigan Cavalry during the Civil War.

Elisha Wesley Harding
Birth:
Jan. 15, 1852
Warsaw
Jefferson County, Pennsylvania
Death:
Jan. 3, 1951net
Corunna
Shiawassee County, Michigan
Burial:
Yerian Cemetery
Vernon
Shiawassee County, Michigan

John W Hallack
Birth:
Oct. 27, 1844
New York
Death:
Jan. 26, 1901
Sparta
Kent County, Michigan
Burial:
Greenwood Cemetery
Sparta
Kent County, Michigan

He died at the age of 44. He was converted when he was 16 years of age, licensed by the Leicester church in 1838 and ordained 10 years later in 1848. He preached at Warsaw, New York for six years and in the Elk County Quarterly Meeting in Pennsylvania. In 1855, they moved to Michigan where he was pastor at Venice and Vernon until his death.

Rev Lyle Henry Hatfield
Birth:
Aug. 14, 1885
Wisconsin
Death:
Oct. 26, 1956
Alpena
Alpena County
Michigan
Burial:
Evergreen Cemetery
Alpena
Alpena County
Michigan
Plot: 24-69 S

Son of William E. HATFIELD, and Wealthy (Rowley) HATFIELD.
He was a student living at Osseo, Hillsdale Co., Mich., when he mar. Nellie May Harter, 20 June 1912. (Her father: Isaac Harter, and mother: Sophia C. Crane.

In 1917 WW I Draft, he was at Sandusky, Sanilac, Michigan, and his occupation was "ordained minister." His Michigan death record stated his occ. was "Ret. Bapt. Minister."

Rev Julius Perry Hewes
Birth:
Mar. 30, 1851
Wisconsin
Death:
Feb. 22, 1907
Hillsdale
Hillsdale County
Michigan
Burial:
Oak Grove Cemetery
Hillsdale
Hillsdale County
Michigan
Plot: SECTION 13 ROW 17

Son of David and Sarah Thompson Hewes, was born at Clayton, Wis., March 30, 1851. His father was killed in the battle at Corinth, Miss., in October, 1862, and his invalid mother was dependent on her only son. With commendable perseverance he applied himself to the work, studying at Lawrence University, Wis., and at Hillsdale College, Mich., graduating from the Theological department at Hillsdale in 1885. He received license to preach in 1872, nine years after his conversion, and was ordained March 8, 1876. His pastorates have been at Pittsford and Bankers, Mich., and

Hortonville, Fairwater and Waupun, Wis. These pastorates have been successful, those at Hortonville and Pittsford having been attended with extensive revivals.

Rev Jonathan Niles Hinckley
Birth:
Jun., 1772
Death:
Jun. 27, 1855
Breedsville
Van Buren County, Michigan
Burial:
Breedsville Cemetery
Breedsville
Van Buren County, Michigan

Rev. Jonathan N. Hinckley was ordained at Russia, NY, in 1806, and settled in Parma, Ohio in 1816. He soon found nine others at Ogden who were ready to unite with him, and a church was organized which soon numbered nearly one hundred. Among the original members of this church were John Hill and Oliver A. Willard, the grandfathers of Miss Frances E. Willard. In 1819 he gathered the Harrisville, Ohio church, which though not itself permanent, was the germ of the Medina Quarterly Meeting. At Milan he organized another church, which stood as a moral light until the Huron Q.M. was built up. He soon returned to New York, however, and continued to labor with the churches of the Monroe Q.M., until 1847, when he removed to Michigan, and remained with the Anthwerp church (Van Buren Q.M.) until his death. He was for many years a leader and a father among the people of his choice."
Inscription:
Rev. Jonathan N. Hinckley
Died June 27, 1855

George Henry Howard
Birth: Apr. 18, 1829
Union
Bloome County, New York
Death:
Feb. 3, 1907
Michigan
Burial:
Ortonville Cemetery
Brandon Gardens
Oakland County,
Michigan

He consecrated his life to God in November, 1857 and received ordination on June 16, 1867 in the Wolf River Quarterly Meeting, Wisconsin. He began his work with the Rosendale, Wisconsin church and then removed to Ortonville, Michigan and later to Lisbon, Michigan. He baptized at 200 converts.

Quarterly Meeting In 1865. He was married in 1870 and the next year became pastor of the Fairfield, Michigan church. After 12 years as a faithful leader there he was again compelled to abandon the work because of poor health.

Edward J. Howes
Birth:
Oct. 17, 1838
Ontario County, New York
Death:
Mar. 16, 1906
Michigan
Burial:
Knauss Cemetery
Kinderhook
Branch County, Michigan
Plot: Lot 92

The family moved to Hillsdale County, Michigan in 1848, and nine years later Howe was converted and united with the North Reading church. He was ordained by the Hillsdale Quarterly Meeting at Cambridge in 1864. His pastorate was with the Salem and Green Oak churches of the Oakland

Thomas Huckins
Birth:
1795
Lee, New Hampshire
Death:
1853
Lexington, Michigan
Burial:
Huckins Cemetery
Croswell
Sanilac County, Michigan

Left an orphan in early life, after serving in the war of 1812, he married and moved to Canada where he joined the first Free Will Baptist church organized in that locality. In 1819 he moved to Dunwick, and later to London. In these places churches were organized and the latter he served as a Deacon until 1827, when he was ordained to the ministry, which occurred soon after. He labored in that vicinity for 10 years gathering three churches and then moved to Lexington, Michigan where his remaining years were spent. Here he soon organized a church to which about 60 members were added during his pastorate.

Alonzo O. Jenne
Birth:
1822
Hartland, Vermont
Death:
1892
Michigan
Burial:
Needmore Cemetery
Needmore
Eaton County,
Michigan

He was converted in 1837; received license to preach in 1847, studying at Whitestown Seminary, New York and was ordained in April, 1853. Much of his ministry was done in the Grand River Quarterly Meeting.

Rev Almon Jones
BIRTH
8 May 1817
Bennington, Wyoming County,
New York
DEATH
28 Oct 1908 (aged 91)
Cedar Springs, Kent County,
Michigan
BURIAL
Greenwood Cemetery
Grand Rapids, Kent County,
Michigan
PLOT   L.20.7

Rev. Almon Jones at age 21 began to preach while attending High School at Varysburg, NY. He was married to Mary C. Hoyle and moved to Raymond, Wis. where he was ordained Jan. 3, 1847, Rev's R.M. Cary, Herman Jenkins, and others conducting the services. He was among the early pioneers in that region and much progress was made during his sixteen years labor there. He had pastoral care of several churches in Wis. and of several in Michigan after removing to that state. He baptized more than 400 persons, and near the close of an active life for God.

Samuel Lamson Julian
Birth:
Sep. 16, 1804
Portsmouth
Rockingham County
New Hampshire
Death:
Mar. 29, 1876
Wayne County, Michigan
Burial:
White Cemetery
Dowagiac
Cass County, Michigan
Plot: Row 6

Samuel Lamson Julian is the eldest child of Andrew Julian and Catherine Lamson. His family was poor and made an honest living by hard work and industry in Portsmouth, New Hampshire. SLJ had distinct recollections of news of significant events of the War of 1812. His father, Andrew, sailed his last voyage during this war. Events recalled were the looming British Fleet off New

Hampshire's coast, at Rye Beach, Perry's victory on Lake Erie, the Battle of Plattsburg, Hall's defeat at Detroit, Andrew Jackson's victory at New Orleans and finally the Declarations of Peace. While he was young 2 brothers died young. Shortly thereafter, his mother, Catherine Lamson, passed away in 1814. These deaths made a significant impression on young Samuel regarding the subject of death. On her deathbed, his mother impressed upon him to seek the Lord. It is something he never forgot and ultimately, he became a traveling preacher.

His father married Mary Muchmore who became his step-mother. At her urging,

As a young adult man, he became acquainted with the Free Will Baptist Church and became a traveling minister for congregation. His journeys took him through New Hampshire, Maine, Illinois and Michigan.

Began to preach in 1830, ordained Brookfield, Nov. 6, 1833. Pastored several churches, and organized churches in Van Buren Co. Mich, and also in Illinois.

He met Nancy L. Hill, daughter of Joshua Hill, Limerick, Maine and was married by Elder S. Burbank on November 2, 1831. They initially set up their home in Shapleigh, Maine.

Samuel had a falling out with the Free Will Baptist Church around 1861. On page 44 of his unpublished autobiography (1875), Samuel says he was "cast out of the synagogue" on the grounds of his "teaching false doctrine such as the non-immortality of the soul and annihilation of the wicked...and other pernicious doctrine contrary to the views of ...the Free Will Baptists denomination.

Anson Green Kalar
Birth:
Nov. 8, 1833
Stamford, Ontario,Canada
Death:
Jan. 31, 1902
Richfield Center,
Genesee County, Michigan
Burial:
Cottage Cemetery
Richfield Center,
Genesee County, Michigan

Parents were William Kalar and Winifred Hawley. A minister of the Freewill Baptist, licensed in April 1877, and pastor in Genesee Quarterly Meeting, Michigan.

Ada Montgomery Kennan
Birth:
Jun. 4, 1839
Madison, Lake County, Ohio
Death:
Apr. 14, 1894
Hillsdale
Hillsdale County, Michigan
Burial:
Oak Grove Cemetery
Hillsdale
Hillsdale County, Michigan

Freewill Baptist minister and pastor. Wife of Rev. George Kennan (1832 - 1905). She was also the mother of Ralph Kennan who was also an effective Free Will Baptist minister.

Moses Rice Kenny
Birth:
Sep. 6, 1816
Townshend
Windham County,
Vermont
Death:
Mar. 25, 1905
Hillsdale
Hillsdale County,
Michigan
Burial:
Oak Grove Cemetery
Hillsdale
Hillsdale County,
Michigan

An ordained Free Will Baptist minister and pastor, born in VT but lived in mid-west for many years. Married Elizabeth "Betsey" Ross, -16 Nov. 1843- Ashtabula County, Ohio. Married Caroline Gage-15 April 1863- Ashtabula County, Ohio.

Samuel Ketcham
Birth:
Feb. 2, 1807
Chautauqua,
New York
Death:
May 6, 1889
Mason, Cass County, Michigan
Burial:
Five Points Cemetery
Edwardsburg
Cass County,
Michigan

He was converted in early manhood and went to Michigan about the time of his marriage to Abigail Pullman, which was consummated on March 13, 1831. She was his companion for more than half a century. On July 15, 1848 he was ordained at Gillead and his ministry was spent in the St. Joseph Valley Quarterly Meeting.

Elijah Kingsbury
Birth:
Unknown
Death:
Aug. 16, 1862
Oakland County, Michigan
Burial:

Kingsbury Cemetery,
Oxford, Oakland County,
Michigan
Plot: Lot 8 Grave 1

Minister and also the father of Rev. Leonard Kingsbury.

Leonard Kingsbury
Birth:
1794
Death:
Oct. 19, 1879
Oakland County, Michigan,
Burial:
Kingsbury Cemetery, Oxford,
Oakland County, Michigan,
Plot: Lot 8 Grave 2

He was converted under the labor of Rev. E. Hannibal. He began to preach and was licensed by the Free Will Baptist Church in Clarkston, New York. He continued to labor in that vicinity until 1834. After which, he moved to the state of Michigan where he was ordained and was accepted into the Oakland quarterly meeting with the Bruce church. His labors

were well known since the established several churches in the Oxford quarterly meeting. He loved the denomination and carefully gave of his time and money and aiding its evangelistic work and benevolent enterprises.

Kingsbury, Rev. Leonard, son of Rev. Elijah Kingsbury, was born in Boonville, N. Y., June 4, 1794, and died at Addison, Mich., Oct. 19, 1879. When quite young he moved to Clarkson, N. Y., where at the age of seventeen he was converted under the labors of Rev. E. Hannibal. He soon began to preach and was licensed by the church. He continued to labor in the vicinity until 1834, when he took up the work in Michigan. In the report for 1834, he appears as an ordained minister coming into the Oakland Q. M. with the Bruce church. In this vicinity his life was spent. God blessed his labors in building up several churches and in organizing the Oxford Q. M. He continued true to his trust till death, though in advanced years he was not active in consequence of the infirmities which came with age. He was a man of perseverance and strong faith in God. He loved the denomination, and cheerfully gave his time and

money in aiding its evangelistic work and its benevolent enterprises.

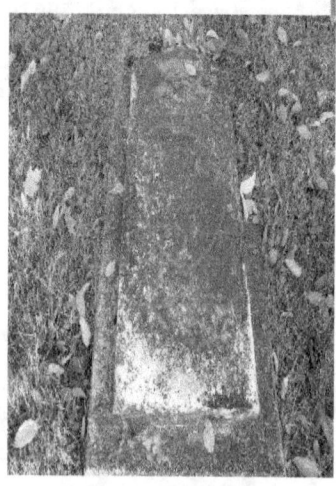

Arnold D. Knight
Birth:
Apr. 8, 1803
Oneida County, New York
Death:
Mar. 18, 1889
Burial:
East Hill Cemetery
Osseo
Hillsdale County, Michigan
Plot: Sec. A, Lot 161

On January 2, 1823 he married Harriet M. Knight. At the age of 18 he was converted and before 1840 he was ordained at the Pittsfield church. He held long pastorates with the Pittsfield, Spencer, and Rochester churches along with some other churches for a brief time. In all these pastorates there were revivals. He baptized over 200 converts and assisted in gathering's six churches.

John Beal Lash
Birth:
Jan. 25, 1841
Athens County,
Ohio
Death:
Jul. 17, 1901
Hillsdale,
Hillsdale County, Michigan
Burial:
Oak Grove Cemetery,
Hillsdale,
Hillsdale County,
Michigan

An ordained Freewill Baptist minister from Ohio, who moved to Michigan and was a great warrior for Christ.

J. B. Leavenworth
Birth:
Jun. 5, 1820
Sandgate, Vermont
Death:
Sep. 20, 1905
Michigan
Burial:
Novi Cemetery
Novi
Oakland County, Michigan

He was born of Puritan ancestry in Vermont but later settled in Novi, Michigan about 1844 and received ordination 18 years later and his ministry was in this vicinity.

Rev Edward Dodge Lewis
Birth:
Feb. 9, 1823
West Windsor
Broome County
New York
Death:
Oct. 2, 1897
Burial:
Oak Grove Cemetery
Hillsdale
Hillsdale County
Michigan
Plot: SECTION 16 ROW 8

Rev. Edward Dodge LEWIS, son of Solomon and Hannah (Weeks) LEWIS, was educated at Farmington Academy and Geauga Seminary, Ohio. Soon after his conversion in 1841, he began to preach, and May 23, 1847, was ordained in Bazetta, Ohio. His first pastorate was as Williamsfield, O., commencing in 1844. After this he labored in Crawford Quarterly Meeting Penn, and the Lake Co. QM, in Ohio. In 1848 he entered the work in Wisconsin, with pastorates at Rutland and Cookville three years; Oregon, three years, organizing a church at Bellville, Johnstown three years; Honey Creek seven years; Warren, Ill, two yrs; Rock Creek three yrs; Prairie City two yrs; Strong's Prairie, Wis, several yrs while regaining health; Bradford 1875-77; Oakfield five yrs; Gobleville, MI, five yrs; and Burnett, Wis.. These churches have been blessed under his labors, with many additions to the membership.

He has held various positions of responsibility and was a member of the Centennial General Conference.

On April 3, 1844, in Ashtabula, O, he was married to Mary P. Woodworth, who received from the Ashtabula, QM, Ohio, license to preach, and engaged with him in the work.

She died in 1863, and in 1865, he was married to Miss Eliza A. Cole, of Providence, R.I., who was graduated from Hillsdale College, Mich, in 1863.

Rev Rick L. Locklear
Birth:
Nov. 5, 1959
Death:
Mar. 28, 2017
Michigan
Burial:
Michigan Memorial Park
Flat Rock
Wayne County, Michigan

He passed away at the age of 57, and had been a resident of Trenton. He was the dear son of Rev. Lloyd and Lois Marie. Cherished husband of Donna. They were married for 36 years. Devoted father of Jessica (Dan) Corne, Jonathan (Stephanie), and Hannah Locklear. "Big Poppy" of Brooks, Vivian, Rickey, and Beckett. Loving brother of Rev. Michael, Bruce, the late Lona, and Towonica. He will also be missed by other dear family members, his church family, and many loving friends. He served as Pastor for the Woodhaven Free Will Baptist Church for 30 years.

David H Lord
Birth:
Aug. 9, 1814
Rumney
Grafton County, New Hampshire
Death:
Jun. 14, 1889
Hillsdale
Hillsdale County, Michigan
Burial:
Oak Grove Cemetery
Hillsdale
Hillsdale County, Michigan

Rev. D.H. Lord was the son of Thomas H. and Louisa (Avery) Lord. He consecrated his life to God in Aug. 1832, and soon began to preach, studying at Parsonfield Seminary, ME, in 1835-36, and on Sept 28, 1836, was ordained to the gospel ministry in the Free Will Baptist Church. He ministered successively to churches in Portsmouth, NH, Springvale, E. Lebanon, and others in Maine, and Newport and Pascoag in RI, in Medina, OH, and in Howard City, MI. He baptized over five hundred converts. His voice having failed, he studied medicine at Brunswick, ME, and Vermont Medical College, graduating in 1849. In Sept. 1838, he married Elmira Clark of Dover, NH, who died seven years later. In 1848, he married Annette M. Merrill, of Parsonfield, ME. After a brief illness at Hillsdale, MI, he died and was buried there. By his wide and benevolent life, he exerted a wide influence for God.

Rev John Stewart Manning
Birth:
Apr. 3, 1813
Whitehall
Washington County
New York
Death:
Jun. 25, 1893
Cairo, Alexander County
Illinois

Burial:
Oak Grove Cemetery
Hillsdale
Hillsdale County, Michigan,
Plot: SECTION 7 ROW 2

John Stewart Manning, son of Ziba Manning and Rachel Polley. He married Maryette Hammond on May 24, 1844. She was born on Jan 24, 1822 in Perrysburg, Cattaraugus, New York, USA. She died on Oct 11, 1899 in Hillsdale, Hillsdale, Michigan,
He founded the Manning Bible Institute in Cairo, Illinois for the Freeman coming up the Mississippi and Underground Railroad.

Joseph William Mauck
Birth:
Aug. 17, 1852
Cheshire
Gallia County,
Ohio
Death:
Jul. 7, 1937
Hillsdale
Hillsdale County, Michigan
Burial:
Oak Grove Cemetery
Hillsdale
Hillsdale County, Michigan

Inscription:
President of Hillsdale College
1902-1922

Dr. Mauck was a graduate of Hillsdale College, Class of 1875, after which he became Professor of Classical Languages at the college. He later served as Chancellor of the University of South Dakota. Dr. Mauck was President of Hillsdale College for 20 years, retiring in 1922 to his beloved home, Sunnycrest, with the title President-Emeritus.

John H Maynard
Birth:
November 29, 1830
Junius, New York
Death:
1905
Burial:
Greenwood Cemetery
Sparta
Kent County, Michigan

After his marriage to Mary Williams in 1853, years later they moved to the state of Michigan. He was ordained in the Hillsdale Quarterly Meeting in January, 1866 with Rev. John Thomas, who had baptized him, preaching the sermon. Most of his pastorates were in the state of Michigan where he served as the Michigan Yearly Meeting clerk for many years and for three times a delegate to the General Conference.

Rev Charles Blunt Mills
Birth:
May 5, 1823
York County, Maine
Death:
Mar. 11, 1896
Mayville
Tuscola County, Michigan
Burial:
Fremont Township Cemetery
Mayville
Tuscola County,Michigan,

Rev. Charles Blunt Mills at his home in Mayville while sitting in his chair during the temporary absence of his wife in attendance at their weekly prayer meeting. He received a good common and high school education, and at an early age he became a minister in the Free Baptist denomination. He was a close student and gave frequent lectures in addition to his regular pastoral work. He removed to Ohio, and from there, in 1856, to Tuscola County, where he bought a farm. He was a State senator in 1869-70 and a representative in 1877 and was judge of probate for Tuscola County eight years. He had been a trustee of Hillsdale College for many years and several years acted as its secretary and treasurer, and was one of the incorporators of the Free Baptist printing house at Dover, N. H. From his close resemblance, both in features and actions to Henry Ward Beecher, he was frequently mistaken for that individual in his earlier days. His address made at Caro in September, 1895, to the large outdoor gathering of the Tuscola County Sunday School Association will long be remembered and his memory cherished by all present on that occasion. He married Ann M. Morrison in 1851.

(Michigan Pioneer & Historical Collections, Vol. 27, 1896.)

Rev Ollie Lafferty, Jr
Birth:
Sep. 7, 1936
Prestonsburg
Floyd County, Kentucky
Death:
Feb. 19, 2016
Ypsilanti
Washtenaw County Michigan
Burial:
Highland Cemetery
Ypsilanti
Washtenaw County Michigan

Lafferty Jr., Rev. Ollie Ypsilanti, MI (Formerly of Prestonsburg, KY, Age 79, went home to be with the Lord following an extended illness. He was the son of Ollie and Lack (DeRossett) Lafferty Sr. On June 1, 1957, he married Peggy S. Day and she survives. Ollie was a former pastor of both Whittaker and Trinity Free Will Baptist Churches, a former member of First Free Will Baptist Church and a current member of Trinity Free Will Baptist Church. He was employed as a machine operator at Ford Motor Company, Ypsilanti plant for 33 years, retiring in 1988 and was a longtime member of the U.A.W. He loved his Lord, family, church, fishing and hunting. The funeral service was at Trinity Free Will Baptist Church, with Pastor Calvin Brown officiating.

Rev John Meighan
Birth:
Mar. 6, 1871
Glasgow City,
Scotland

Death:
Jul. 16, 1928
Hillsdale
Hillsdale County
Michigan
Burial:
Oak Grove Cemetery
Hillsdale
Hillsdale County
Michigan
Plot: SECTION 19E
ROW 13EW

Note: 1904-1921 Minister - 1921-1928 Professor Of Religion At Hillsdale College.

Rev. Thomas Ross McCullough
Birth:
Dec. 22, 1950
Royal Oak
Oakland County
Michigan
Death:
Aug. 11, 2017
Michigan,
Burial:

White Chapel Memorial Park
Cemetery
Troy
Oakland County
Michigan

THOMAS ROSS, born at 11 p.m. to Calvin and Grace McCullough.

Tom grew up in Royal Oak and graduated from Kimball High School in 1969. He attended Oakland University for 2 years playing golf and hockey for the University. Through the influence of Pastor Raymond Riggs, Assistant Pastor Bill Robinson, and Youth Pastor Leroy Welch, Tom accepted the Lord on January 25, 1970. His life now took a new direction and Tom attended Free Will Baptist Bible College (1971-74) in Nashville studying Bible and Pastoral Training, where his senior year he served as Student Body President.

He worked at Central school and Church with Patty Underhill whom he married in March, 1977. In 1979 Tom and Patty were approved for missionary service. They spent the 1980's in language school and serving on the mission field in France. In 1988-89 while on deputation he completed his thesis and earned a MA at CIU. Then they returned to France to serve at the church in St. Nazaire.

Tom and Patty separated from the Missions Department in 1994. Ian Ross was born February 14, 1994 and joined the McCullough Family June 20, 1994. Tom worked at Central

Church as an assistant to the Pastor.

In 1996 Tom joined the faculty of his alma mater, FWBBC, where he taught Missions until 2002. In October, 2002 Patty, Ian and Tom returned to Michigan to begin his pastoral career at Central. In his selfless love for the growth of the church and the building of the Kingdom of God, Tom encouraged the congregation at Central to hire a younger man of God. He helped to transition the leadership role of Pastor to Jacob Riggs and in 2015 retired from Central. In March, 2015 he joined Riverside Fellowship Church in Clinton Township as assistant Pastor to Steve Thrasher, II.

In his never ending commitment to the Great Commission, Go into all the world and preach the Gospel. . ., Tom has set up "The Tom and Patty McCullough scholarship fund for mission students at Welch College" (formerly known as FWBBC). To honor his final request a contribution to the Foundation, instead of flowers, would be greatly appreciated.

Spouse: Patty J. Underhill McCullough (1953 - 2004)

Patty J. Underhill McCullough
Birth: Mar. 7, 1953
Detroit
Wayne County
Michigan, USA
Death: Dec. 18, 2004
Royal Oak
Oakland County
Michigan, USA
Burial:
White Chapel Memorial Park
Cemetery
Troy
Oakland County
Michigan

Patty J. Mc Cullough, age 51, died at William Beaumont Hospital, Royal Oak, Michigan. Mrs. McCullough earned a bachelor's degree. She and her husband, The Rev. Thomas McCullough, were former missionaries in France for 15years.

Rev John Bascom McMinn
Birth: 1873
Illinois

Death: Oct. 11, 1949
Flint
Genesee County
Michigan Burial:
Rich Township Cemetery
Mayville
Lapeer County
Michigan

Married 4-1897 Mary Rice Chaplain in World War I Veteran. Rev. J. B. McMinn, 76, passed away Tuesday Oct. 11th, at Hurley Hospital, Flint, as the result of injuries received Friday afternoon, Oct. 7th, when his car and one driven by Walter H. Smithling, of Davison, collided on M-15 at Lapeer Road, just south of Davison.

John Bascom McMinn was born in Illinois, the son of Mr. and Mrs. Thomas O. McMinn. In. April 1897, he was united in marriage to Mary Rice, and to this union five children were born, one son Randall, died in infancy.

Mr. McMinn had been pastor of the Baptist Church here for the past 15 years, and resigned only a month ago. He was active in civic affairs and was the (first president of the local Rotary Club when it was organized in 1942. He was a Chaplain in the U, S. Army in France in World War One. He held pastorates in Illinois,

Kansas, Nebraska and Wisconsin before coming to Michigan.

Funeral services, were held at the Mayville Baptist Church, Rev. Orviie Williams of Dearborn officiated, assisted by Rev. William Collier, local Pastor.

Samuel A. J. Moody
Birth:
Feb. 25, 1825
Chautauqua County, New York
Death:
1891
Michigan
Burial:
Fairfield Cemetery,Adrian
Lenawee County, Michigan

He was born in Chautauqua Co. New York, Feb. 26 1825. His parents were Samuel and Martha (Thompson) Moody. He married Roxey E. Emmery in 1859, and had six children. He was converted in 1839, and received ordination May 26, 1861.He ministered to the Liberty and First and Second Augusta churches in Michigan and engaged in revival work at Rose, but for several years was hindered in the work because of disease. He also received certification to teach school in 1855, in the Lenwanee Co. schools.

Inscription:
"In God's Care"

REV Gideon H Moon
BIRTH
26 Jul 1814
Rensselaer County, New York, USA
DEATH
1 Feb 1892 (aged 77)
Hillsdale County, Michigan, USA
BURIAL
Oak Grove Cemetery
Hillsdale, Hillsdale County, Michigan, USA
PLOT   SECTION 14 ROW 1

Gideon H Moon, son of James Moon and Anna Dodge, was born in 1814 in Rensselaer County, New York, USA. He died on February 01, 1892 in Hillsdale County Michigan. He married Mary Burke Smith. She was born in 1820 in Newark, Licking, Ohio, USA. She died in 1911 in Marion,

Marion County, Ohio, USA.

Moon, Rev. Gideon H., son of S. and Annie (Dodge) Moon, was born in Williamstown, N. Y., July 26, 1814. In May, 1841, he was married to Mary B. Smith. Of their ten children, six yet live and two have entered the ministry. He was converted in 1832, license to preach was granted in 1837, and ordination was received in October, 1840. He labored with much devotion and success as pastor of several churches in the Marion Q. M., Ohio, then in the Licking Q. M., and in the vicinity. In this work his health was impaired but the churches were strengthened. In 1872 he moved to Illinois, where he immediately took charge of two churches and soon organized the Big Mound church of the Wayne Q. M. He continued in pastoral work until 1881, since which he has preached occasionally. His baptisms number about two hundred and fifty. His preaching is remembered for its close reasoning, sometimes rising to eloquence.

Marcus Mugg
Birth:
Aug. 12, 1809
Yates County, N. Y.
Death:
Jun. 23, 1865
Mason, Mich.
Burial:
Five Points Cemetery
Edwardsburg, Cass County, Michigan
Plot: Section 1, Row 8, Stone 2

Marcus was the son of Rev. John Mugg, and died at aged 56 years. His conversion took place in York, Ohio, where he soon began to preach and was ordained June 6, 1840. He spent most of his ministerial life with the churches of the Huron and Seneca Q. M's, Ohio, where his general influence and exemplary life were appreciated. Some twelve years before his death he moved to Michigan, where bereavement and sickness awaited him. His wife passed to a better world and his eldest son was slain in the war. But the sustaining grace of God was present.

Rev A. A. Myers
Birth:
1838
Death:
1924
Burial:
Oak Grove Cemetery
Hillsdale
Hillsdale County, Michigan
Plot: SECTION 18 ROW 32EW

Erastus W Norton
Birth:
Sep. 9, 1818
Richmond, Ontario County, New York
Death:
Aug. 9, 1887
Sparta, Kent County, Michigan
Burial:
Greenwood Cemetery
Sparta Kent County, Michigan
Plot: O-2-1

Rev. Norton's parents were John and Norma (Short) NORTON. He married 1) Minerva Gardener, Feb. 14, 1839, and 2) Laura A. Compton, July 17, 1851.He was converted when twelve years of age, and ordained in the Freewill Baptist church in Michigan when twenty-three years (ca 1841). He went to Kent County in 1850, where his principal work in the ministry was done. The Sparta and Lisbon churches enjoyed his services many years, and both built houses of worship during his pastorate. He was strongly denominational, a good preacher, and an energetic business man. His wife and ten children were left to mourn his passing.

William R Norton
Birth:
February 12, 1822
Richmond, New York
Death:
1902
Burial:
Rose Cemetery
Bath
Clinton County, Michigan

He was converted in 1843 and the same year received licensed to preach. He moved to Michigan in November of that year and commenced to labor in the Oakland Quarterly Meeting where he was ordained in 1848. In 1854 he moved to Clinton County and also the Lansing Quarterly Meeting where he organized the Bath church which he served for 22 years. He later became a missionary in the vicinity of Boyne City in the northern peninsular of Michigan. He had two sons both of whom graduated from Hillsdale College with Walter E., being a soldier in the Civil War and William A., a successful lawyer.

Rev Benjamin E Parker
Birth:
Feb. 26, 1806
Brutus
Cayuga County
New York
Death:
Mar. 20, 1877
Addison
Lenawee County
Michigan
Burial:
Hillside Cemetery
Addison
Lenawee County
Michigan

Son of Thomas and Sarah Elliott Parker and Brother of Rev Seth C Parker.

Linus S Parmelee
Birth:
August 20, 1815
Spafford, New York
Death:
1895
Burial:
Maplewood Cemetery
Old Reading
Hillsdale County, Michigan
Plot: Old Part Sec E Lot 30

On May 3, 1835 he married Julia A. Jones and their son, Horatio, became a trustee of Hillsdale College, Michigan. Linus was converted the year following his marriage. In 1847 he received licensed to preach and that next year was ordained. He ministered the Salford, Ontario, Canada church for seven years, and two years the Innerskip church which he organized. He then moved to Reading, Michigan and assisted in organizing that church and was its pastor for 21 years. He also assisted in organizing the Woodbridge and West Reading churches and served them also as pastor. Four of these churches build houses of worship during his pastorates and he had baptized more than 210 converts. He also spent some time in Chicago and raised several thousand dollars for the interest of Free Will Baptist. He also raised $18,000 for the Hillsdale College from which he also served as a trustee for 15 years.

Michael G Pett
Birth:
1836, England
Death:
Apr., 1901
Michigan
Burial:
Carson City Cemetery
Carson City
Montcalm County
Michigan

PETT, Rev. M.G. (Michael G.), The children from their births, parents could have lived in Illinois. A dau, Anna (Pett) Gamble, 1871-1904 d. in Calif. Calif Dth record states her parent's names. A christening record of 04 Nov. 1836, Trinity, Ely, Cambridge, Eng. for Rev. Michael G, states his parents were Henry and Mary ? PETT. His tombstone has the title "Rev" on it.

Dr. Jeremiah Phillips
Birth:
Jan. 5, 1812
Plainfield Center,
Otsego County, New York
Death:
Dec. 9, 1879
Hillsdale,
Hillsdale County, Michigan
Burial:
Oak Grove Cemetery,
Hillsdale,
Hillsdale County, Michigan

He studied at Hamilton Literary and Theological Seminary, N.Y; ordained at Plainfield, NY, Sep. 2, 1835. Was among the very first missionaries for Free Will Baptists, going to India in 1835, aged twenty-three, with his colleague, Rev. Eli Noyes, and founded the Free Baptist Mission in Orissa, India. He began work among the Santals, an aboriginal tribe, reduced their language to writing, and also prepared a dictionary and grammar, and translated the gospels and other portions of the Bible. He married Mary Spaulding Beede in 1835, who died soon after arriving in India. In 1839, he married Mary Anne Grinditch, Serapore, India, who also died. Thirdly in 1841, mar. Hannah W. (Cummings) who had gone to India at twenty-two years of age, died there in her ninetieth year, having had but two furloughs during the intervening sixty-seven years.

Dr. Jeremiah Phillips was the father of fourteen children, eleven of whom lived to mature age, six of whom and three granddaughters became workers in the same field, while five remaining in America were nearly, or quite all active workers for missions.

On his retirement from the field in 1879, with health completely shattered by privations and strenuous labors during one of India's terrible famines, the Lieutenant-Governor of Bengal addressed to him a letter in which he said he could not allow him to retire without expressing his high appreciation of the valuable service he had rendered to India.

His eldest son, a medical doctor, James L. Philips, spent twenty-five years in the same field and was the Field Secretary of the India Sunday-School Union, in whose service he remained until in 1895.

Also, a daughter, Dr. Nellie M. Phillips, and Dr. Thomas Wesley Burkholder, a son-in-law, were medical missionaries. Eleven of Dr. Phillips' family are buried in India, including his last wife, Hannah Cummings Phillips, while Dr. Phillips himself, and those of two missionary daughters and one daughter-in-law, rest in Oak Grove Cemetery. One daughter, Mrs. Julia P. Burkholder (widow of Dr. T.W. Burkholder), served 50 years as a missionary in India. A fine brick church now stands in Khargpur, India, a memorial to Dr. Phillips, erected in 1906-07 by Mr. and Mrs. I.L. Stone, (Harriet Phillips Stone) of Battle Creek, the latter a daughter of Dr. Phillips, and for twenty-six years a member of the mission. This family did great service for God in helping the poor and down-trodden, and gained for themselves, a great reward.

**Dr.
Nellie Maria Phillips**

Birth:
Jun. 15, 1852,
India
Death:
Mar. 7, 1906
Rochester,
Olmsted County,
Minnesota
Burial:
Oak Grove Cemetery,
Hillsdale,
Hillsdale County,
Michigan

She graduated from Hillsdale College, MI in June 1875. She engaged in teaching and the study of medicine until 1881, graduating at that time from Adelbert Medical College, Cleveland, Ohio. She served with her parents and a rather large, extended family as a medical missionary to India, from 1881 to 1903. Dr. Phillips died in Rochester, MN.

Ida Orissa Phillips
Birth:
Jan. 24, 1856
Death:
Jul. 5, 1889
Winnebago,
Faribault County, Minnesota
Burial:
Oak Grove Cemetery, Hillsdale,
Hillsdale County, Michigan

Daughter of Jeremiah L. Phillips, DD, and Hanna (Cummings) Phillips, Free Will Baptist missionaries to Orissa Province India. She graduated from Hillsdale College, MI. in 1877 and was a missionary to India from 1877-1889, at the time of her death, at age 32 yrs and 5 months. She came from an extended family of medical missionaries and ministers. Her mother lies buried in India with other family members there. Ida came to U.S. at age 16, probably to attend college, in Dec. 30, 1870 with a clergyman's family, Rev. Obadiah B. Batchelder, M.D., who worked with the Phillips family in India. Most info is from a book, pub. 1912, *"Jeremiah Phillips, DD, Family Missionaries to India"* by Harriet Phillips Stone.)

Mary R *Sayles* Phillips
Birth:
Unknown
Death:
Feb. 6, 1911
Battle Creek,
Calhoun County, Michigan
Burial:
Oak Grove Cemetery, Hillsdale,
Hillsdale County Michigan

Married James L. Phillips, M.D., at Pasoag, R.I., Aug. 10, 1864, a Free

Will Baptist missionary to India. She died at 73 years, after serving with her husband in India. He died there in 1895.

Mary Anne *Phillips* Platts
Birth:
Feb. 20, 1842,'
India
Death:
Apr. 25, 1911
Winnebago,
Faribault County, Minnesota
Burial:
Oak Grove Cemetery,
Hillsdale,
Hillsdale County, Michigan,
Plot: Row 3

Mary Anne was the daughter of Free Will Baptist missionaries to India, Dr. Jeremiah Phillips, and Mary Anne (Grimditch) Phillips She married R. Gilbert Platts, MD, Dec. 15, 1866, in Brittany NY. She studied at Whitestown Seminary, NY and Prairie City Academy, Illinois, and New Hampton Seminary, N.H. They served at missionaries with her extended family in Orissa Province, India,

where her husband died at the early age of 34 yrs.

Richard Gilbert Platts
Birth:
Nov. 4, 1838
Old Saybrook,
Middlesex County, Connecticut,
Death:
Jan. 3, 1873,
India
Burial:
Oak Grove Cemetery,
Hillsdale,
Hillsdale County, Michigan,
Plot: Plot: Row 3

Gilbert Platts, M.D. was a student of Hillsdale College, MI, and was graduated at Buffalo Medical College, N.Y., Feb. 1866, as a physician. He married Mary Anne Phillips, the daughter of Jeremiah Phillips, D.D., and Mary Anne Grimditch Phillips, Free Will Baptist missionaries to India, on Dec. 15, 1866, at Bethany, NY. Death occurred in India in January 1873, and presumed re-interment in 1874, in Oak Grove Cem. as Feb. 1, 1874, is shown as date of burial He died a young man at 34 years of age. His wife is also interred in Oak Grove. The children are buried at the Riverview Memorial Cemetery in Ft. Pierce, Florida.

Rev Freedom Randall
Birth:
Apr. 10, 1842
Burlington, Michigan
Death:
May 21, 1915
Tekonsha
Calhoun County
Michigan
Burial:
Riverside Cemetery
Tekonsha
Calhoun County, Michigan

His parents were Gilbert and Alma (Howe) Randall. He consecrated his life to God in Jan. 1868, and received ordination in Dec. 1877. He had pastoral care of the Penn church two years, the Hadley's Corners church three years, and the Leslie church two years, and in 1881, settled with the Cook's Prairie church, to which thirty-eight were added under his ministry the past year.

July 3, 1866, he was married to Melissa S. Downs, who died in 1872. They had a son, Hazen C. Randall, 1870-1936, MI In 1874he married Mary O. Smith.

Rev Delavan B Reed
Birth:
Jun. 12, 1855
Sardinia
Erie County, New York
Death:
Sep. 27, 1932
Manton
Wexford County, Michigan
Burial:
Fairview Cemetery, Manton
Wexford County Michigan
Plot: Section 2, Lot 525

Rev. Delevan Bloodgood REED was the fifth child and only son of Lewis B. and Hannah (Quackenbush) REED. His parents were members of the Free Baptist Church in NY and in 1879 He entered the ministry. After study in Griffith Institute, Springville, NY, He entered Hillsdale College in Mich. in Jan. 1881, and graduated from the classical course in 1888, and from the theological course in 1889.

He was president of the Theadelphic Society in the spring of 1886 and won the prize in he oratorical contest of 1885.

In 1888 he was elected to the Chair Of Ecclesiastical History in the theological department of the college, and pursued a post-graduate course of study with that work in view.He was ordained at Wheatland, Mich, about 1881, and has ministered to the Pittsford, Wheatland, and Pittsford Village churches in Michigan while pursuing his studies; and also, for a brief time, to the Johnstown and Oakland churches in Wisconsin.

Chauncey Reynolds
Birth:
August 28, 1805
Argyle, New York
Death:
1890
Burial:
Oak Grove Cemetery
Hillsdale
Hillsdale County, Michigan

In the winter of 1819 the family moved to Bethany, New York.

During that first year he became interested in religion, but delayed baptism until 1827. He went to Michigan in 1828 and was married to Sarah Harper, October 30, 1828. He was ordained at the Grand River Quarterly Meeting in October, 1845 and soon organized the church and Shiawasasee County. He also organized a church and Du Plain, Clinton County, and another in North Plains, and assisted in the work in other places. He was a trustee of Michigan Central College at Spring Arbor and served also as a trustee at Hillsdale College for 20 years and he served as a delegate to the Gen. Conference in 1853.

William T. Risner
Birth:
1847
Prussia
Death:
1919
Burial:
Novi Cemetery
Novi
Oakland County, Michigan

He married Sarah Hammond in 1868. In 1874 he was led to Christ's and licensed to preach was granted four years later. He received his ordination on February 14, 1883. His pastorates were in Michigan.

J. C. Robinson
Birth:
April 14, 1836
Harrison County,
Ohio
Death:
1922
Burial:
Oak Grove Cemetery
Coldwater
Branch County, Michigan

His parents migrated from Virginia to Ohio where he turned of God in August, 1851. Seven years later he was licensed to preach having received his education Albany University, Ohio. On August 24, 1862 he was ordained by Rev. H. J. Carr and others. His labors have been in Ohio, Minnesota, Illinois, Wisconsin and Michigan. He has organized five churches and baptized 125 people.

E B Rolf
Birth:
Vermont
Death:
Nov. 16, 1872
Bristol,
Indiana
Burial:
East Union Cemetery
Union
Cass County, Michigan

After his conversion he joined the Sodus, New York church. The Holland Purchase Conference granted him a license to preach in 1843 and his ordination took place on July 12, 1844. 21 years of his ministry was spent with the Galen and Savanna churches of Wayne Quarterly Meeting, New York. About 1865 he assisted in organizing the church at Porter, Michigan and remained its pastor until he died.

His manhood was spent in Hillsdale County, Mich., where he engaged in the work of the ministry for some twenty years before his death. He was faithful in duty, and none could leave a better reputation for sincere piety.

Charles A Shattuck
Birth:
Feb. 19, 1815
Leyden,
Mass.,
Death:
Apr. 9, 1887
Burial:
Mount Hope Cemetery
Litchfield,
Hillsdale County,
Michigan
Plot: Section 9 Row 1 Lot 3

John Silvernail
Birth:
November 17, 1828
Greene County, New York
Death:
1917
Burial:
Brigham Cemetery
Monroe County, Michigan

He was brought to Christ in 1852 and was ordained in April 1867. His ministry was mainly in Michigan.

Nor pain, nor death can enter there.

Tilton E. Smith
Birth: 1840
Death:
Feb. 4, 1890
Lapeer
Lapeer County
Michigan,
Burial:
Mount Hope Cemetery
Lapeer
Lapeer County
Michigan

Free Will Baptist Minister and Civil War Veteran, Corporal 33 New York Infantry Company-E
Enlisted: May 9, 1861
Discharged: June 2, 1863
Enlisted In: Yorktown, New York

Rev Sheldon Smith
Birth:
Apr. 14, 1836
Elbridge
Onondaga County
New York
Death:
May 17, 1892
Van Buren County
Michigan
Burial:
Arlington Hill Cemetery
Bangor
Van Buren County
Michigan
Plot: Sect. 1

Rev. Sheldon Smith, son of Bliss and Priscilla (Rounds) SMITH, was married to Miss Emily Hakes Feb. 14, 1856.
In 1882, she died, and he afterwards married Miss Susan Stevens, May 29, 1883, Van Buren Co. MI.
In September 1873, he was ordained by the church of God. In 1885, he united with the Free Baptists, and was pastor of the church at Corey Hill, Van Buren County, Mich. In 1882 he was elected department chaplain of the G.A.R. of the state of Michigan, having served in the late war in Co. H, 19th NY H.A. Regiment.

O Thou Who Choosest For Thy Share

*The World, And What The World
Calls Fair,
Take All That It Can Give Or Lend,
But Know That Death Is At The End*

Lonnie H. Sparks
Birth:
Dec. 14, 1930
Davis
Murray County, Oklahoma
Death:
Jun. 26, 2014
Edwardsburg
Cass County, Michigan
Burial:
Edwardsburg Cemetery
Edwardsburg
Cass County, Michigan

No one could have foreseen this second child of Lewis and Linnie Sparks, now deceased, Lewis Sparks Jr., would travel the world working to break the spiritual and financial poverty of those living in the jungles of West Africa (Cote d'Ivorie); in the cities of Europe (Alcala de Henares and Santurce Spain); and in the U.S., (primarily in Elkhart and briefly in Oklahoma and South Carolina) before making his home in Edwardsburg. He was born in the Depression Era in Davis, Oklahoma. His 56 years of ministry were preceded by a time of rebellion against God, when Lonnie, wanting to escape his own family's poverty, went to school to assure himself a financially secure future. Ironically, Lonnie, who was studying to be an automobile engineer, was brought back to obedience to Christ by an automobile accident that nearly took his life. Lonnie then and there surrendered himself to God's will, embracing the cross and whatever sacrifice, financial and otherwise situation, that might cost him. In the summer of 1954, after having secured a B.A. from Free Will Baptist College (now Welch College) in Nashville,TN and in Winona Lake, IN for a summer scholarship course, surrendered to a call to the mission field after hearing a message by Oswald J. Smith, in the Billy Sunday Tabernacle. That decision sealed the deal for Anita J. Kaminsky, who made the decision to break up with Lonnie, and not accept his proposal of marriage, since he had never mentioned the mission field, and she knew in her heart of hearts that she had to be a missionary. They were married that summer on Aug. 15,

1954 in Elkhart, IN. They pastored two churches in Oklahoma in 1954-1955, before moving to Columbia, SC, where they attended Columbia Bible College (now University) in the 1955-1956 school year, where they pastored two churches while Lonnie was securing a Masters in Missions. On Dec. 22, 1956, they left from New York Harbor for language study in Switzerland, where they spent a whole year learning the French language. In Jan. 1958, they left for the Ivory Coast, studying and learning the Twi language (Ghana) and then Koulango (Ivory Coast). On Feb. 14, 1959, their son Paul was born (since deceased) in Dembrokro. During their stay in Africa, Lonnie established a church in Goumere, and had many more preaching points. Also, sensing the need for the Koulango Tribe to have the Word of God in their language, he came back to the U.S. on a furlough, where son Noel was born in 1962, and studied at Wycliffe Summer School of Linguistics on the campus of the University of Oklahoma in Norman, OK, before moving on to get his Masters in Linguistics from the University of Michigan, Ann Arbor in 1963. Lonnie, back in Africa, reduced the language to writing, wrote a school primmer, so the children could study in their native language, and, most importantly, translated the New Testament into the Koulango language. From 1974-1997, they served as missionaries to Spain,

where they opened two churches in Alcala de Henares (Madrid) and Santurce (Vizcaya), and was the case with Africa, saw many people come to faith in Jesus Christ. In 1997, Lonnie and Anita came home to "retire", but through work in the now defunct La Vanture Plastics Corporation, came into contact with a burgeoning Hispanic community. What started as a home Bible Study, ended up becoming the Primera Inglesia Bautist Libre of Elkhart, IN, where he served as pastor until Alzheimer's forced him to truly retire.

A Service at the Primera Inglesia Bautista Libre (their church), of a Life Well Lived began with some of his co-pastors officiating, including, but not limited to, his son, Pastor Noel Sparks, the church pastor, Pastor Robert Helms and other associates, Pastor Lonnie Palmer and Pastor Mark Riggs. The funeral procession went to Edwardsburg (MI) Cemetery, where was laid to rest next to his deceased son, Pastor Paul Sparks.

Paul M. Sparks
Birth:
1959
Ivory Coast, West Africa
Death:
1992
Indianapolis, Indiana
Burial:
Edwardsburg Cemetery,
Edwardsburg,
Cass County, Michigan

He was the minister of the Antlers Free Will Baptist Church in Oklahoma at the time of his passing. He had formerly served churches in Winona Lake and Elkhart, Indiana and before was a missionary to Spain.

Federal Alcander Stanford
Birth:
March 15, 1815
Oneida County,
New York
Death:
1901
Burial:
Mount Hope Cemetery
Middleville
Barry County,
Michigan

He was married to Miss Sophia Hicks in 1838. His conversion took place in 1832 and he was ordained in February, 1854. His ministry was spent in Pennsylvania, Ohio and Michigan with the longest continuous pastorate being in watch in Michigan. In September 1873, he was ordained by the church of God. In 1885, he united with the Free Baptists, and pastor of the church at Corey Hill, Van Buren County, Mich. In 1882 he was elected department chaplain of the G.A.R. of the state of Michigan, having served in the late war in Co. H, 19th NY H.A. Regiment.

Norman Starr

Birth:
Unknown
Death:
Sep. 16, 1865
Burial:
Hart Cemetery
New Baltimore
Macomb County
Michigan

He was an ordained minister connected with the Southfield church of the Oakland Quarterly Meeting, Michigan as early as 1856. He remained with this church until about 1859 when he became pastor of the Chesterfield and Lenox church of that Oxford Quarterly Meeting where he remained until his death. Note: age 42 yrs.

Rev Henry T. St Clair

Birth:
Aug. 26, 1824
England
Death:
Jan. 13, 1908
Fenton
Genesee County, Michigan
Burial:
Oakwood Cemetery
Fenton
Genesee County, Michigan

Henry was a Minister. Father is Howard St Clair from England, mother unknown. ST CLAIR, Rev. Henry T. I could find few records. But there is a death cert on his memorial which gives his occ: Minister;

John Thomas

Birth:
Unknown
Death:
Oct. 10, 1874
Burial:
Fairfield Cemetery
Adrian, Lenawee County, Michigan
Thomas, a native of New York, while yet young consecrated

himself to God and his work. Soon after receiving license in Royalton, N. Y., he commenced laboring in Michigan, receiving ordination at the Michigan Central Q. M. Feb. 23, 1839. There were then few Free Baptist churches in the state, but giving himself, soul and body, time and talents, to his work, neither the poverty of the churches nor the. Roughness of the roads weakened his courage or diminished his fervor. Many log cabins were cheered by his genial presence, many rough schoolhouses were made houses of God and gates of heaven to converted souls. After laboring several years as an evangelist, he settled as pastor and spent nearly twenty-five years with the Wheatland and Fairfield churches of the Bean Creek (later Hillsdale) Q. M. His sermons were short and earnest, sprinkled at times with a little natural eccentricity and wit, and full of love. His sermons were practical and forcible, his life godly and earnest, and the whole enveloped in a cheerful, affectionate spirit, which seemed to be the most forcible element of his nature. After spending a little time in labor at Blackberry, Ill., he returned to the scenes of his former labors, and died Oct. IO, 1874, aged 58 years. He was an early and constant friend of Hillsdale College, and for some time a trustee. He was the Pastor of Fairfield Baptist Church from 1864-1870.

Nelson Thomas
Birth:
1820
Death:
Aug. 7, 1848
Constantine, Michigan
Burial:
Five Points Cemetery
Edwardsburg
Cass County, Michigan
Plot: Section 1, Row 8, Stone 10
He was 27 years old at his death which came only three years after his ordination. However during that three years he organized three churches and was a preacher of much promise.

Rev John Fletcher Tree
BIRTH
22 Jun 1844
St. Marys, Perth County, Ontario, Canada
DEATH

8 Dec 1936 (aged 92)
Webster, Washtenaw County,
Michigan,
BURIAL
Forest Lawn Cemetery
Dexter, Washtenaw County,
Michigan

An ordained minister who came to Michigan and became pastor of several churches during his ministry, some he organized, and engaged in revivals.

Rev William P. VanWormer
BIRTH   3 Dec 1855
Gilead, Branch County, Michigan,
USA
DEATH   1913 (aged 57–58)
BURIAL
Oak Grove Cemetery
Hillsdale, Hillsdale County,
Michigan, USA
PLOT   SECTION 10 ROW 5

Joseph Harvey Walrath
Birth:
Jan. 14, 1847
Canajoharie
Montgomery County, New York
Death:
Aug. 31, 1892
Michigan
Burial:
Oak Grove Cemetery

Hillsdale
Hillsdale County, Michigan
Plot: Section 14

In 1847 he married Miss L. M. Mount. Entering Hillsdale College in 1871, he passed through both the academicals and theological departments graduating in 1878. He was ordained by the Hillsdale Quarterly Meeting in September, 1876 and had the pastoral care of many churches within this state of Michigan, Iowa, South Dakota and Wisconsin. For four years he was secretary treasurer of the Wisconsin Home Mission Board. Other positions which he occupied were: agent of the Free Baptist Western Association, State Agent and Evangelist of the Iowa Yearly Meeting, and was the Corresponding Editor of *The Free Baptist* from its beginning to February 15, 1888. In pastoral and evangelistic work and in his life of official work for the denomination he was successful.

Death Has No Strength

John T. Ward
Birth:
Jan. 20, 1847
Norway,
Herkimer County, New York
Death:
Dec. 9, 1918
Yokohama, Kanagawa, Japan
Burial:
Oak Grove Cemetery, Hillsdale
Hillsdale County, Michigan

He graduated from Whitestown Seminary in 1867, from Hillsdale in 1870, and from Andover Theological Seminary in 1873. While a student in Hillsdale he was a member of the Amphictyon society and the Hillsdale chapter of Delta Tau Delta fraternity, being one of the seven charter members of the latter when it was founded in 1867. He received ordination to the ministry in the Freewill Baptist church on Dec. 14, 1873. As pastor, Dr. Ward served several of the leading Free Baptist Churches in Ashland, NH; Georgiaville, R.I; Park Street, Providence, RI, and Jackson, MI, and was prominent in the activities of the denomination. He was elected as delegate to the national conference and was on educational boards, and served six years on the Home Mission Board. He was also a member of the General Conference Board and trustee of Hillsdale College from 1889-1898. He became editor and manager of *"The Free Baptist"* at Minneapolis, the first religious paper in the northwest, founded by Rev. A. A. Smith, a former pastor of the College Church in Hillsdale. He managed and edited the paper with distinct efficiency for a number of years and was instrumental in merging it into *"The Morning Star"* in Boston. During his service as pastor and editor he and two fellow clergymen edited *"The Free Baptist Encyclopedia,"* a large volume of significant ecclesiastic and historic value, which passed to the sole control of Dr. Ward shortly after he and the one surviving collaborator received it from the press and bindery. He had positive convictions on the doctrines and practices of the Church, but was of a practical vision, and was one of the most consistent advocates of co-operation of the denominations in their foreign missions, federation and union at home and abroad, openly supporting the organic union of the Baptists and Free Baptists which was wrought out while he was in Hillsdale. He entered the faculty of Hillsdale College in 1898 where he served until 1913, with one intervening It is knowing that God WILL!year of leave of absence which he and his wife spent with Mrs. Phelps in Japan. His subjects were theology and homiletics. During a part of the residence of the family in Hillsdale, the daughter Mary, the only child and a graduate of the University of Minnesota, was an instructor in Hillsdale College, and was active in the religious and club life of the college and city. On her marriage to Mr. Phelps they went to Japan, where he is one of the most prominent of the international secretaries of the Young Men's Christian Assn. Probably remembered now more as the co-author of *"Free Baptist Cyclopedia"* with Gideon Burgess, pub. 1889.

Rev William S Warren
BIRTH
11 Jan 1826
Detroit, Wayne County, Michigan
DEATH
25 Nov 1892 (aged 66)
Hillsdale County, Michigan
BURIAL
Churches Corners Cemetery
Wheatland, Hillsdale County, Michigan

Obit: Dec. 2, 1892:"Rev. William S. Warren, Churches Corners, d. here Nov. 25th, aged 66 yrs. Received academic education. At age 19 began preaching the word in connection with teaching. Served in the ministry over thirty-five (35) years with the Freewill Baptists. Nine years ago, he was ordained as pastor of Baptist church of Dundee. For over six years has been pastor of Churches Corners church.

The loss of his wife led him to resign the pastorate, but he accepted a call in Indiana. He married Catherine Steadman, 11 Aug. 1892 at Hudson, Hillsdale, MI, she age 56 (b, 1834) and he 66y, b. 1826. Her father: David Wormly.

Abraham H Whitaker
Birth:
June 9, 1845
Kirklin, Indiana
Death:
1917
Burial:
Bankers Cemetery
Hillsdale County, Michigan
Plot: Sec 1 Row 2 Lot 16

On January 1, 1868 he married Sarah Ellen Balcom. Brother Whitaker was converted 11 years of age, was a student at Centerburg Academy, Ohio and four years at Hillsdale College in Michigan and received his ordination in January, 1871. He pastored many churches in Michigan, and, also churches in Ohio and Wisconsin. He nearly all of these revivals were enjoyed under his labor. He organized three churches and baptized about 200 converts. He was active in temperance and every good work, and was highly esteemed among his brethren both as a preacher and a pastor.

Nor pain, nor death can enter there.

Elder Samuel Whitcomb
Birth:
June I, 1788
Lisbon, N. H
Death:
April 7, 1867
Clarendon, Mich
Burial:
Cook's Prairie Cemetery
Clarendon, Calhoun County,
Michigan

Aug. 5, 1813, he married Miss Nancy Jacobs. In 1816 he was thoroughly converted. Soon after he moved to Lyons, N. Y., and joined the Presbyterian Church. Disagreeing with them in doctrine, in December, 1819, he united with the Free Baptist church in his place. He moved to Hartland in April, 1822, and soon to Shelby, where he organized a church in 1824, and was its pastor till he moved to Michigan in 1838. Here the next year he organized the Cook's Prairie church in Clarendon, where he retained his membership till death. Oct.10, 1844, his wife died, and he afterwards married Miss Lydia Cowles, of Burlington, Mich. He was in sympathy with all denominational enterprises, a safe counselor, a practical preacher. He was once a member of General Conference.

William E. Whitney
Birth:
1812
Penfield, Monroe County,
New York
Death:

Sep. 17, 1893 Leslie Ingham
County,
Michigan
Burial:
Woodlawn Cemetery Leslie
Ingham County Michigan

He began his Christian life in 1832, moved to Canada in 1834, commenced to preach in 1844, and was ordained a Free Will Baptist minister in 1846. He moved to Michigan in 1849 and worked with various churches there. He served as a soldier in the Civil War in the Mich. 12th Infantry, Co G, in the early part of the war, and re-enlisted in 1864. He lost a limb, but on his return resumed the work of the ministry and was a faithful servant of God.

Samuel Wire
Birth:
1786
Goshen, Conn
Death:
Jun. 6, 1870
Commerce, Mich.
Burial:
Wixom Cemetery,
Wixom, Oakland County
Michigan

His father served in the British army and was present at the defeat of Braddock; he also served in the army of the Revolution. Brother Wire moved to western New York in early manhood, and was baptized with his wife by Elder Z. Dean in May, 1819. Immediately he began to preach and was ordained the same year. In July of that year he and Elder Dean sought out David Marks and introduced him to his life of usefulness, and from that time Brother Wire was active in carrying forward the work. His labors were abundant and successful in western New York and northern Pennsylvania until 1833. When he removed to northeastern Ohio, and labored in the Ohio and Pennsylvania Y. M. Subsequently he returned to New York, where in 1843 his companion of thirty-eight year was parted from him. He afterwards married 'Widow Colby of Sodus. N. Y., and removed to Michigan, where his remaining years were spent. Brother Wire was a man of unusual natural ability and of extraordinary energy. Which made his life an exceedingly active one. For many years he is prominently mentioned in the field of his labors, and he did much to strengthen the denomination. His love of preaching was intense, and in the days of his strength, his soul burning with holy zeal, there was sometimes a power in his sermons which was well-nigh irresistible.

Elder Joseph Woodman
Birth:
Feb. 12, 1790
Barrington
Strafford County
New Hampshire
Death:
Apr. 2, 1879
Paw Paw
Van Buren County
Michigan
Burial:
Bangs Cemetery
Paw Paw
Van Buren County
Michigan

Elder Joseph Woodman was born in Barrington, N. H., Feb. 12, 1790. When quite young, his father, John Woodman, with his family, became a pioneer settler in Caledonia Co., Vt. Joseph was the second child, and eldest son in the family, and in early life he developed those active qualities of labor, perseverance, and prudence, which crowned his life with success and honor. He was married to Tryphena Johnson, of the same county, Jan. 1, 1810, with whom he lived a happy union fifty-three years, she dies June 14, 1863, in the seventy-second year of her age, having had ten children, six of whom still survive. Riley, the eldest son, resides in Powhatan, Kan., the other five, viz.: David Woodman (2d), J. J. Woodman, Mrs. Joseph Luce, Mrs. Freeman Ruggles, and Mrs. H. P. Nelson, are residents of Van Buren County.

Soon after his marriage he, with his wife, joined the FreeWill

Baptist Church. Earnest in his religious convictions, he soon to the labor of his hands joined that of the ministry and engaged in preaching the gospel. In the spring of 1831 he sold the farm (among the hills) in Sutton, on which he had lived several years, and which he cleared and improved with his own hands, also the saw-mill which he built on the stream near his residence, and in July of that year emigrated to Western New York, and settled on a farm in Riga, Monroe Co., where he resided until the spring of 1835, when he with his family moved to Michigan, and settled upon the land which he located and which became his future home, on the Territorial Road in the township of Antwerp, east of and adjoining the village of Paw Paw. He was the first white settler and built the first log house and the first frame barn in the township. His log house, built in three days and finished ready for occupancy, and into which he moved his family on the 10th day of May, 1835, was built on the spot now occupied by the fine residence of his youngest son, Hon. J. J. Woodman, to whom he sold all of his farm in 1861, except forty acres on which his residence stood, which he built in 1838, and in which he lived forty-one years, and until his death, April 2, 1879, at the advanced age of eighty-nine years, one month, and twenty-one days.

When he settled upon his farm there was but one small frame house, three log cabins, and a sawmill on the territory now occupied by the beautiful and flourishing village of Paw Paw. There being no church of his faith near him at the time, he united with the Protestant Methodists, and was soon after ordained, and was actively engaged in the ministry until within a few years of his death, when advancing age compelled him to retire from the pulpit and active duties of a long and useful life, and seek the quiet and comfortable surroundings of his home and fireside. His second wife, Mrs. Mary Osmer, to whom he was married in the winter of 1883, faithfully ministered to him in his declining years.

MR. JOSEPH WOODMAN.